Wow! This book will make you want to jump up and down for joy, and shout the victory as we begin to know the power and importance of our identity in Christ. Upon reading this book "I AM The God Kind," YOU can say without a doubt who you are in Christ and will BOLDY declare "I am The God Kind!"

Pastor Mary Cooper
Associate Pastor, Victory Christian Fellowship
Founder, Daughters of Esther Ministry

"I Am the God Kind" is a treasure hunting book that seeks but one treasure; the Kingdom of God. But unlike treasure maps that have hidden secrets, false leads, and blind alleys; this book has an honest elegance about it that will lead people to the peace that is Jesus Christ. It will take you on a joyful path to your relationship with Jesus, the words of His Father, and a gathering of the Holy Spirit that desires to fill you.

Gloria's words are obviously not hers but are the inspiration of the Holy Spirit that so wants us to find the passage to eternal happiness in one of the many rooms Jesus has prepared for us in His Father's house. Embrace the beauty of Jesus Christ as you walk through these chapters and let them fill you with comfort that we have a God who loves us.

John Radell
Faith and Freedom Coalition
Mid-Atlantic Regional Director

What Christian Leaders Are Saying About This Book.....

This is a fantastic book! Reading this book can help you reclaim your identity and walk in victory in your daily life. Gloria states that a Christian who does not understand their identify in Christ will forfeit the abundant life Jesus purchased for them. This is because identify breaks the power of fear, depression, guilt, shame, addiction and every kind of bondage.

She shares how we can redefine our identify with Christ; like Saul, the persecutor of the church, who became apostle Paul, the man who did more to spread the gospel of Jesus around the world than any other apostle. This same power of God's voice causes us to see ourselves through His eyes, and births a self-redefinition that transforms us into that same image.

This book will encourage you to not let the enemy deceive you because God loves and cares for you. After reading this book you can proclaim "I AM a child of God! I am an offspring of God!"

Dr. Phyllis J. Arno
Co-Founder, National Christian Counselors Association
Sarasota, Florida

I recommend this book as an effective manual on our identity in Christ for all believers, churches, and Christian groups. *"THE GOD KIND"*, unravels some of the major questions about our identity in Christ which has plagued Christians for so long. For this reason, I believe that it has come at an auspicious time in the history of the Church. It is an outstanding, well-researched, informative, substantive and highly readable book. Every page will inspire readers to take what is rightfully theirs as children of God, so that they would experience a major move of God in their lives!

This is an amazing book about how Christians can become all that God has purposed for them to be, according to His word. It is loaded with useful biblical information for those who want to enjoy all the benefits of knowing who they are in Christ. Gloria uses scriptures and great life examples to take readers on a fascinating journey about the 'fabulous riches' we are entitled to as children of God.

As you read this book, not only will you discover the true meaning of our identity in Christ, but you will also know and understand how to live a victorious life as a child of Almighty God. Gloria makes it clear that we are redeemed, chosen, valued, forgiven, loved, and fully accepted by Christ, not because of anything we have done but because of who He is and what He did for us.

Congrats for a great work, Gloria!

Kwaku Marfo
Senior Pastor, International Central Gospel Church, Exaltation Temple
Newark, Delaware

This is a must read for those who hunger and thirst for more and more of the God life. Wanting and desiring to know who they are in Christ and becoming familiar with the tactics and strategies of the enemy to STOP the plan and purposes of God in our lives.

"I Am the God Kind" certainly will open the eyes of believers to their identity in Christ, to learn how to walk in the power of God, and become all that we are created to be as we operate in the power of the risen Christ.

Gloria tells us how Satan tries to rob us of our inheritance, when we don't know who we are in Christ. I was impressed by the stories of Eva & the Peladi brothers who lived grueling lives of poverty and deprivation, completely oblivious to the fact that they were extremely wealthy. Ever heard the story of the hard-boiled egg in relation to The Father, Son and the Holy Ghost? What a powerful revelation!

Gloria gives us examples of those believers who identify in self and those who identify in God, and what a contrast between the two! It's a powerful story of our righteousness, authority and dominion. I loved when Gloria said, "Every time we say yes to sin, we are denying our identify in Christ".

I AM

THE GOD KIND

LIVING IN THE REALITY OF YOUR IDENTITY IN CHRIST

I AM
THE GOD KIND

LIVING IN THE REALITY OF YOUR IDENTITY IN CHRIST

PLUS

PROCLAMATIONS TO BUILD CONFIDENCE, CHRIST ESTEEM AND GODLY SELF-IMAGE

GLORIA GODSON

THE GOD KIND, LIVING IN THE REALITY OF YOUR IDENTITY IN CHRIST

Plus 31 Day Proclamations to Build Confidence, Christ Esteem and Godly Self-Image.

LifeWork Ministries, Inc.
P. O. Box 56
Townsend, DE 19734

www.lifeworkministries.org
lifeworkministriesinc@gmail.com

LifeWork Press
© 2021 by Gloria Godson

Cover photo: Original photography by Rhema Godson.

All rights reserved solely by the author. No part of this book may be reproduced in any form without the permission of the author. For permission requests, contact [gloriagodson1@gmail.com].

Unless otherwise indicated, Scripture quotations taken from the Holy Bible, New Living Translation (NLT). Copyright ©1996, 2004, 2007 by Tyndale House Foundation. Used by permission of Tyndale House Publishers, Inc.

Scripture quotations taken from the New King James Version (NKJV)–*public domain*.

Printed in the United States of America.

ISBN: 9798527937633

Dedicated

to

Emmanuel, Timothy, and Rhema

and

my Friend and Partner, Holy Spirit

and

My many trials and tribulations that have compelled an authentic Christ identity

TABLE OF CONTENTS

What Leaders Are Saying About This Book…

Introduction

Chapter 1— Fabulous Fortunes……………………………...1
Chapter 2— You be You……………………………………11
Chapter 3—Your Identity…………………………………...26
Chapter 4— The Identity Parable ………………………….42
Chapter 5— Mistaken Identity ……………………………..53
Chapter 6— Identity is Foundational ……………………...60
Chapter 7 —The Inner Man………………………………...71
Chapter 8— The God Kind ………………………………...87
Chapter 9 — The Divine DNA ……………………………..94
Chapter 10—God Shaped, The Divine DNA in Us ……...115
Chapter 11— Proof of Identity…………………………….122
Chapter 12— Your identity Will Be Challenged…………132
Chapter 13— Your Identity in Christ ……………………..137
Chapter 14— False Identity ………………………………149
Chapter 15— Rejection …………………………………...159
The Missing Link - Proclamations ……………………….168

Afterword…………………………………………………...200
Notes …………………………………………………….. 202

INTRODUCTION

In over three decades of my personal walk with Christ, prophetic prayer ministry and service to the body of Christ, I do not know of one single thing that has as much impact on the life and outcomes of a believer, as knowing who they are in Christ, walking in that reality, and having their identity, self-definition, and personal affirmation in Christ alone.

This is the one thing that guarantees and underlies victory for every Christian in their personal walk of faith, or conversely, spells doom and defeat when lacking or under developed. When a Christian gets a revelation of what it means to be a child of the Most-High God, it strengthens their resolve to win and empowers them to overcome sin, shame, guilt and condemnation. Knowing who they are in Christ breaks the power of addiction, low self-esteem and emotional bondage; and positions them for a winning walk. It powers and empowers their vision of the future.

A Christian who does not understand, embrace or walk in the reality of their identity in Christ will forfeit the abundant life Jesus purchased for them and live a life riddled with fear, defeat, sickness, poverty, mental and emotional bondage, and oppression.

Identity is powerful!

- Identity breaks the power of fear
- Identity breaks the power of depression
- Identity breaks the power of guilt

- Identity breaks the power of shame
- Identity breaks the power of addiction
- Identity breaks the power of every kind of bondage

When you know who you are in Christ, the devil can no longer intimidate, terrorize or bind you; sin can no longer be your master, and boss you around; chains that once held you captive have no option but to fall off, because you can no longer be bound; when you know, really know, believe, and appropriate the glorious truth of who you are in Christ! Knowing who you are in Christ is the single most liberating and empowering truth a Christian can embrace. It sets you on the trajectory to overwhelming victory!

This book makes a compelling case for our identity in Christ. It highlights the God-kind attributes that set us apart as children of God; illuminates our hearts to understand and locate ourselves in God's plan; challenges and shifts our perspectives; outlines a clear path for us to partner with God in His plan for our planet; and lights up the runway for us to take flight and become all that God created us to be.

I AM
THE GOD KIND

LIVING IN THE REALITY OF YOUR IDENTITY IN CHRIST

CHAPTER 1
FABULOUS FORTUNES

In 2008, Eva Paole, a retired Argentine maid living in poverty, learned that she had inherited the whopping sum of $40 million. Unbeknownst to her, she was the daughter of baron Rufino Otero, who died in 1983 and had no children with his wife. Until then, Eva had thought that she was the daughter of her mother, Josefa, and her partner. Though her mother had never told Eva who her father was, she had heard rumors that she might be the baron's daughter. Through research and talking to her mom's friends and relatives, Eva came to believe that Rufino was her father, and took DNA tests which confirmed that she was indeed the daughter of the powerful land owner.

In May 2010, in Budapest Hungary, two brothers, Zsolt and Geza Peladi, a pair of penniless down and outs, inherited a share of a $7 billion fortune. The Peladi brothers were so poor they lived in a cave outside Budapest, and sold scrap materials and other junk they scavenged in the streets. Lo and behold, after a life of abject poverty, both men, then in their forties, and their sister who lives in America, learned that they inherited their grandmother's massive fortune. They knew their mother came from a wealthy family, but she had severed ties with her family long before her death. The Peladi brothers learned of their good fortune after they were contacted by lawyers handling the estate of their maternal grandmother, who died in Germany and left no next of kin. Under

German law direct descendants are automatically entitled to a share of any estate, which in this case passed from their dead mother to them.

Both Eva and the Peladi brothers had lived grueling lives of poverty and deprivation, completely oblivious to the fact that they were extremely wealthy. Eva was practically nobility, but she lived, worked and retired as a maid. She would have died in poverty, if she had not taken steps to ascertain her true identity. That discovery unlocked a $40 million inheritance and catapulted her from rags to riches. Imagine how she would have felt when she got the news. Imagine even further, if she had not taken steps to investigate the rumors about her ancestry; and had lived and died, so rich, but alas, so poor! Think of all the years she went without, scraping out a meager existence as a maid, while her $40 million inheritance lay unclaimed! The only thing that she needed to do to receive her inheritance was to confirm her identity as the daughter of baron Otero.

Similarly, the Peladi brothers would have died as they lived, homeless and penniless. Imagine how they felt, when they went from living in a cave one day, scrounging in the streets for scraps to sell for a buck; to becoming billionaires overnight. For both Eva and the Peladi brothers, they didn't have to 'DO' anything to earn their inheritance. It came with their ancestry. It was their birthright. But they almost missed out on this incredible reality, because they did not know who they were, or more importantly, whose they were. The only action they needed to take to qualify for their fabulous fortunes was to know, confirm, claim and enforce their true identity.

Rags to Riches

Rags to riches stories are a favorite literary staple the world over! From Cinderella, to Jane Eyre, to The Cash Boy; rags to riches is a common archetype in literature and popular culture. Something in our humanity connects deeply with any situation in which the underdog wins, or a person rises from abysmal poverty to towering wealth or from absolute obscurity to dizzying heights of fame and fortune. These stories inspire hope and faith in children and adults alike to believe that anything is possible.

The Bible tells the ultimate, true, rags to riches story; a dramatic love story of how Jesus left His deity and mansions above, to come to planet earth to rescue fallen humanity trapped in sin, shame, and bondage by the devil. He loved us, and wanted us for His own. But we were hopelessly bound and enslaved by the enemy, the devil; and his side kick, the flesh. There was no other way to save us than through His own death. So, He died a gruesome death on Calvary's cross to pay the ransom for our freedom. John 3:16 says it best, "For God so loved the world that He gave His only begotten son, that whosoever believes in Him will not perish, but have everlasting life". Jesus moved us from rags to riches, from death to life, from bondage to freedom, and from slavery to sonship!

King Solomon's Lament

In Ecclesiastes 10:7, King Solomon laments, "I have seen slaves on horseback, while princes walk on the ground like servants." This is an anomaly, a sorry sight to see! Slaves riding on horseback, at a time when horses were the privilege of kings and nobles; while princes, the sons of kings, who should by right of birth be on horseback, are consigned to, or choose either by omission or commission, to walk on the ground like servants. This unfortunate scenario sounds like a scene right out of a blockbuster Hollywood "Trading Places" type of movie, except that this is a real life drama played out in the lives of millions of Christians daily.

The Bible declares that as many as receive Christ, He gives them the power to become sons of God (John 1:12). Revelation 1:6 says that God has made us 'kings and priests". We are royalty! This is our birthright. We don't have to DO anything to qualify. We were already qualified by God when He adopted us as His children. All we have to do is to believe and appropriate the truth that we are sons and daughters of Almighty God. But sad to say, this is not the reality of so many Christians. Like Eva, many Christians are living beneath their lofty inheritance.

Romans 8:17 states that, as children of God, we are heirs of God and joint heirs with Christ. Imagine that! We have access to everything that makes God, God. As His children, we are inheritors of all of God's mammoth and limitless resources and estate; and have authority in three realms, in heaven, on the earth, and under the earth! But that truth is not evident in the lives of many Christians. Their lives are a far cry from this glorious reality. Like the princes in Solomon's lament, they still walk the streets in poverty, sickness, affliction and deprivation, while non-believers ride on horseback.

Galatians 4:1-5 explains why:

> As long as the heir is a child and under age, he does not differ from a slave, although he is the master of all the estate; But he is under guardians and administrators *or* trustees until the date fixed by his father. So, we also, when we were minors, were kept like slaves under and subject to the elementary teachings of a system of external observations and regulations.

The scripture is clear! As long as we remain infants or minors in our Christian walk, we will never live in the reality of our vast spiritual inheritance in Christ. The reason Jesus came was to purchase our freedom, pay our ransom, and atone for our sins, so that we might be adopted into God's family, have the rights of sonship conferred upon us, and walk in our inheritance as sons and daughters of God. Christ has done His part. Our part is to know, believe, claim and enforce our inheritance.

In Hosea 4:6, God said, "My people perish from a lack of knowledge." In no area is this more true than the actualization of the inheritance rights and privileges that accompany our identity in Christ. Many Christians have perished from a lack of knowledge of who they are in Christ. Ignorance of their true identity has allowed the devil to rob them blind! This is because our identity in Christ is our access to all that God has and is. It is our key to heaven's vault. We unlock God's provisions of grace, favor, health, wealth, abundance and overflow through knowing God and who we are in Him.

> *Our identity in God is like deep roots that keep us anchored, connects us to our life source- God, and keeps us strong and resilient.*

Go to The Front Desk

I heard the story of a famous preacher who went to visit Alzheimer's patients at a nursing home. He went around and greeted the residents. Many regularly watch him on TV and were very glad to see him. He walked up to one woman. She didn't appear to recognize him, so he asked, "Do you know who I am?" She said, "No, but if you go to the front desk, they can tell you". This is a humorous story, but sadly true. Many people don't know who they are.

Sometimes, even the most ardent believers have seasons when they appear lost in the identity wasteland. They confront challenging situations that cause them to stagger, flounder, doubt, and question who they are in Christ. The good news is that even when we forget who we are, God doesn't. We are His children and our identity is secure in Him. We have His DNA, and are partakers of His divine nature. All we need to do is to "go to the front desk" and be reminded of who we are. The Holy Spirit who lives in us is our confirmation that we belong to God (Galatians 4:6). Plus, we can look in the Bible and it tells us in vivid detail who we are. A popular TV minister begins his sermons with a declaration, "This is my Bible, I am what it says I am, I have what it says I have and I can do what it says I can do." This is a declaration that is well worth repeating. The Bible is the mirror for our spirit and tells us who we are and what we have in Christ.

Not knowing who they are, and whose they are, has led many Christians into falling for the cheap lure of sin, settling for less than their inheritance or living on scraps and crumbs instead of sitting at the table and feasting on God's bounty. Others have given in to the lies of the devil or capitulated to the pressure from the world and their base fleshly desires, simply because they don't know, or have forgotten that sin is not their true nature. The truth is that in Christ, we have a new nature created in righteousness and true holiness (Ephesians 4:24). The good news is that, anytime we remember who we are and recalibrate; we can arise, reinstate, and reclaim all that is ours in Christ.

God knows who we are, and He sees us in Christ. The devil also knows who we are, he just doesn't want us to know it, or to live in the victory that comes from that knowledge. His whole scheme is to lie, deceive, and cajole Christians into seeing themselves as less than they are and by so doing, to settle for less that God intended for them to have and forfeit their massive inheritance in God.

Your Identity Is Your Anchor

I have counseled many people who have been Christians for a long time, and are strong and faithful followers of Christ, living lives of Christian discipline, service, and devotion to the Lord until inevitably, "life happens". Sooner or later, something happens that throws them off their rockers and they are shaken, lose their moorings, and are unable to regain their spiritual stability, confidence, equilibrium, and balance. A divorce, death of a loved one, a traumatic diagnosis, financial loss, and so on, can destabilize and dislocate a Christian, but only to the extent to which they do not know, understand, or believe the truth about their identity in Christ.

Conversely, knowing who you are in Christ and having your identity in Him is the sure and steadfast anchor for your soul in the storms of life. It grounds, stabilizes and settles you! It is the tap root that grows down deep into the soil of the person, character, and resources of God to provide a firm, unshakable, foundation and nourishment in a season of severe drought or wilderness experience. It secures you to the Rock of Ages and makes you immovable.

Jeremiah 17:5-8 draws a sharp contrast between someone who has their identity in themselves, and another person whose identity is in the Lord.

IDENTITY IN SELF	**IDENTITY IN GOD**
Cursed	Blessed
Trust in man	Trust in the Lord
Rely on human strength	God is their hope and confidence
Turn their hearts away from the Lord	Like trees planted by the river with roots that reach deep into the water
Stunted shrubs in the desert	Not bothered by the desert heat
No hope for the future	Not worried by long months of drought
Will live in the barren wilderness	Never stop producing fruit

Our identity in God are like deep roots that keep us anchored, connects us to our life source - God, and keeps us strong and resilient.

In Matthew 7:24-27, Jesus told the story of the wise and foolish builders, two people who each built a house. Jesus said, "anyone who hears my teaching and *applies it to his life* can be compared to a wise man who built his house on an unshakeable foundation." This is the key to a life built on durable, hardy, unshakeable, rock solid, foundation - taking the word of God, receiving it as truth, believing it, and applying it with specificity to your life or whatever situation you are dealing with. When you do that, you dock into the Rock of Ages; the Chief Cornerstone; the eternal foundation laid by God Himself, which is Christ and Christ alone (1 Corinthians 3:11).

Over time, consistent application of the word of God to your life will ensure that the entire infrastructure of your life is built on the word of God. You will have a strong identity that is rooted and grounded in Christ Himself. You become unshakeable! The inevitable rain of life will fall, the floods will come, the fierce winds will blow, but the house or life that is built on and rooted in Christ will remain firm. It's like the old hymn:

Will your anchor hold in the storms of life?
When the clouds unfold their wings of strife
When the strong tides lift and the cables strain
Will your anchor hold or firm remain?

We have an anchor that keeps the soul

Steadfast and sure while the billows roll,

Fastened to the rock, which cannot move,

Grounded firm and deep in the savior's love.

Your identity in Christ is your anchor in the storms of life!

CHAPTER 2
YOU BE YOU

In 2017, a man calling himself Prince Khalid Bin Al-Saud, and claiming to be a member of the ultra-wealthy Saudi royal family, entered into talks with real estate developers to make a $400 million investment in an iconic luxury hotel on Miami Beach.

He looked the part of a royal Saudi prince! He wore diamond rings, Cartier bracelets and Rolex watches, as well as traditional Middle Eastern garments such as a white thobe and a red-and-white ghutra headdress. He lived in the penthouse condo of a luxury high-rise on Fisher Island, the richest zip code in the U.S, with an average income of $2.5 million as of 2015. This exclusive private island neighborhood located off the coast of Miami, has been home to celebrity residents like Oprah Winfrey and Andre Agassi.

Khalid drove a 2016 Ferrari with diplomatic license plates and had a security detail. He also sported a Bentley and a Rolls Royce, and traveled on yachts and private jets. He showed off his fabulous lifestyle on social media, posting Instagram photos of his luxury vehicles, diamond-encrusted jewelry, Rolex watches and lavishly adorned cat, named Foxy.

There was just one problem: Prince Khalid Bin Al-Saud was no prince at all. He was actually a con-man named Anthony Gignac. He was born in Bogota Colombia and was orphaned at an early age. A nice middle class family from Michigan adopted him and his brother.

At six years of age, he told his first grade teacher the bogus story that his family owned the largest hotel in town. From then on until his latest arrest in 2017, he pretended to be different royal princes from Saudi Arabia – Prince Mishaal, Prince Omar Khasoggi, Prince Adnan Khashoggi, and Khalid Bin Al Saud. Under his various aliases, he successfully ripped off high end stores like Louis Vuitton and Neiman Marcus; as well as luxury hotels and resorts; of hundreds of thousands of dollars, and spent years in jail. But instead of quitting, he honed his skills for the biggest score of all.

With his latest con, he was able to rip off the rich and famous to the tune of over $8 million, by offering to sell them pieces of his non-existent stake in the Saudi Aramco oil company at a discount, ahead of the company's planned public offering. Unfortunately, as the Department of Justice said in a statement in May 2019, "Those funds were not put into business opportunities, legitimate investments, or any interest-yielding source. Instead, Gignac used the money to finance his lavish lifestyle, including Ferraris, Rolls-Royces, yachts, expensive jewelry, designer clothing, travel on private jets, and a two-bedroom property on Fisher Island".

In March 2019, then 48-year-old Gignac pleaded guilty to charges of impersonating a foreign diplomat, aggravated identity theft, wire fraud and conspiracy to commit wire fraud. Two months later, he was sentenced to more than 18 years in federal prison.

Why the Charade?

Why would a person pretend to be somebody else? Because they place a higher value on that other person's identity than they do on theirs; or because using the other person's identity offers them cover and anonymity; or gives them access to wealth, status, and power that would normally be beyond their reach in their own identity. They want to be "somebody". Usually somebody with clout; or sometimes, somebody with assets more mundane and practical like good credit. They like good credit and the opportunities it affords, but do not want to take the time, do the work, and make the sacrifices necessary to establish one themselves. They want the easy way out. Their false identity affords them the opportunity, albeit temporary, to purchase, gain or do things today, that they would normally not be able to do in their own capacity. So, they are willing to live a lie, even though they know that path is illegal, short lived and fraught with difficulties.

Anthony Gignac impersonated members of the Saudi Royal Family, not because he wanted to be Saudi or an actual member of the royal family. He did not want the responsibilities, duties and challenges that come with being a member of the royal family. He wanted only the perks and privileges. He wanted to enjoy the wealth, status and prestige without the work and sacrifice.

Why would sophisticated, well educated, wealthy and intelligent people believe Anthony Gignac? Because he played another person so well that he was credible at it. The only problem is that he lost himself in the process. At 48, he had spent nearly all of his adult life pretending to be somebody else. The world never got to see or know the real Anthony Gignac, the man who God created him to be. If he was so great at playing somebody that he was not, imagine how awesome he would have been if he simply focused on being

Anthony Gignac. Think of it; there is only one Anthony Gignac in the entire world, and he was the only one most qualified, anointed, empowered and wired to be that person! He would have been a phenomenal Anthony Gignac! His best attempt at being a Saudi prince netted him $8 million, but landed him in prison. He did a great job, but on a wrong assignment. Only God knows the dizzying heights he could have achieved if he focused on being the best Anthony Gignac he could be. But he squandered that opportunity. What a tragic waste!

Probably none of us would ever be an Anthony Gignac, but we engage in various forms of pretense daily, from innocent disguises like makeup, SPANX and hair weave, to elaborate lies that we tell ourselves and others. These lies create a wrong self-image on the inside of us, and the duplicity and incongruence compromise our personal integrity.

So, the same question applies to us. Why do we tell and believe lies about ourselves? Why is it that we hide ourselves or wish that we were someone else? Why do we spend so much of our emotional energy, as well as physical and financial resources trying to look like or be like someone else? Why do people torture themselves with looking at Instagram images of others who make them loathe them selves and despise their body image? Why is it that at church, we covet what other people have, their spouse, friends, physical appearance, title, position or influence; and why is it that we spend our money buying designer clothes, shoes, bags and other accessories, because we think that it will confer on us some sort of distinction, acceptability, or status?

The reason is that we do not like the real us, and think that no one would either, if they knew us. So, we soul distance and social distance. We keep others at arm's length, camouflage, and adopt different personas to be the person we think others want us to be, so as to be accepted by them, or simply to survive in the world we live in. We disguise ourselves in order to fit in with certain people or to belong with them.

But the truth is that God did not call us to fit in. He called us to stand out! We are uniquely hand crafted by God, and He is well aware of our quirks and deficiencies. In fact, they are part of His plan and the story He has outlined for our lives. Someone has said that with God, our oddities become our commodities. So, it's okay to be you. In fact, that is the purpose for which God made you. You are fully licensed by your creator to be you, and He has a plan and many blessings for the real you, not the person you pretend to be. So, go ahead and fulfill God's purpose. Be your own celebrated, authentic, and distinguished self! You qualify!

You are the only person qualified to be you.

Out of Place

Trying to be someone or something that God has not called you to be can take a huge toll on you personally and on the body of Christ. Several years ago, God showed me the body of Christ and the sad and terrible damage that not being our true selves can do. The Bible says that as "The human body has many parts, but the many parts make up one whole body. So it is with the body of Christ" (1 Corinthians 12:12). Just like all the parts of the body have a proper place and an ordained role in the body, likewise, every Christian has a proper place and an ordained role in the body of Christ. Our personal fulfillment and wellbeing in life is highly dependent on finding our set place, rightful role, and proper placement in the body.

Some years ago, the Lord showed me a human body where the heart was outside the body, beating desperately. The body was bloodied and in the agonizing throes of death and dying. It was terrifying! The Lord asked me whether I had ever seen a living human heart out in the open, outside of the body? I said no. He asked me whether it was normal for the heart to be seen publicly, I said no. He then asked me what circumstances would justify or warrant the heart being outside of the body? I thought a little bit and said, "well, it would have to be a super critical situation, like if the person was undergoing open heart surgery". The Lord then said that what I just saw was the condition of many churches. They are in critical condition because the vital organs were out of place, exposed and draining the life out of the body. Individuals whom God had called and ordained to be the heart, kidneys, lungs, and so on, had abandoned their proper place and assignment, climbed out of the body cavity and were trying desperately to be the face, mouth, eyes, and other visible parts of the body. They wanted visibility, they wanted to be seen, to have a microphone and be on stage. They did this because they despised their assigned place and thought that their role was obscure and insignificant. They mis-interpreted visible as important. They feel overlooked and taken for granted, and want the public acclaim and applause that comes with visible roles.

However, as soon as they move outside their proper position and divine placement, they put the whole body into a critical condition, where it is vulnerable and exposed to the enemy! They did not know that their role, though hidden, was extremely crucial. The body can survive without lips, eyes, nose or ears, but it cannot survive without the heart, kidneys and all the internal organs that nobody ever sees.

What is more, in moving out of their place, they are stressed and unhappy, and put everybody else under tremendous stress. Their God ordained function in the body is neglected and that puts the body in mortal danger. And since the body already has a person that God ordained to be the mouth, face, eyes, and so on, their role usurpation is very disruptive to the body. It causes friction, strife and contention, which compromises the body's constitution, health and wellness. Needless to say, they are not very good at their self-ordained roles; impair the ability of others to function in their appointed roles, and cause division in the body. They also cause a lot of confusion and conflict. Imagine, for example, two mouths, speaking different messages, at the same time. People are distracted, misled, and divided, and the church is wide open for attack by the enemy. Simply stated, being out of place in the body compromises the health and wellbeing of the members individually, and the health and mission of the church.

That was a very sobering revelation! Since that time, I have cherished my non-visible roles in the body of Christ. Obscurity helps to clarify and purify our motives, and keeps us humble and focused on serving the Lord alone. So, you be you! Be who God made you to be, a proud original, and not a cheap copy. Stay, grow and bloom where God planted you. That's where you fit perfectly! As you stay in your place and do your own specially assigned work, it helps the other parts of the body to grow, so that the whole body is healthy and growing and full of love (Ephesians 4:16).

Like Anthony Gignac, it is not enough to do a great job, you must do a great job on the right assignment, your own assignment. God rewards you for doing what you are called to do. He blesses and rewards you for being you. That is your assignment, to be you; the very best, most authentic you possible. You are the only you in the world. You are the only one most qualified, anointed, empowered and wired to be you! So, you be you; a phenomenal, outstanding, off-the-hook, you, because only you can! Like Anthony Gignac, impersonating somebody else or usurping another person's role in the church is out of order, will leave you unfulfilled, and will land you in trouble with both man and God.

> *It is not enough to do a great job, you must do a great job on the right assignment, your own assignment.*

Self-Acceptance

Self-acceptance is to know, approve, affirm and believe in oneself; to regard oneself as normal, proper, and okay; to view oneself as acceptable. It is the exhaustive, subjective and realistic assessment of oneself that concludes with a satisfactory and affirmative nod. It is your personal validation of yourself; the favorable culmination of an honest, comprehensive, internal review of you; your temperament, personality, values, interests, strengths, weaknesses, deficiencies, abilities, dreams, proclivities, insecurities and quirks. It is your ability to embrace the whole you, good, bad and ugly, and be comfortable in that embrace.

Self-acceptance is critical because if you don't accept yourself, you will not be able to live with confidence or authenticity; you will not be able to achieve congruence; and you will go through life as a misfit. Lack of self-acceptance is at the root of most internal and external conflicts. It breeds low self-esteem, a poor self-image and is a magnet for rejection. Accepting yourself means letting go of your secret resentment against God for not designing you the way you would have designed yourself. It combats jealousy, envy, competition and many other negative emotions and mindsets. Self-acceptance helps you to make peace with yourself, acknowledge your shortcomings and get down to the business of being you. When you do, you'll find that the world is full of unique people just like you, who are imperfect, and who have quirks, personality traits, and interests similar to yours. Self-acceptance is truth telling. It is speaking the truth to yourself, about yourself. It's giving yourself permission to be you, without qualification or apology. It is being able to genuinely and confidently laugh at yourself. It's saying to yourself, "I am me, and that's great". Genuine self-acceptance is truly liberating!

Lack of self-acceptance on the other hand is an exhausting way to live! It is like forever running, and always losing the race. When you don't accept yourself, you have that gnawing feeling at the back of your mind that you don't measure up, that everyone else is better than you, and today may be the day that your inadequacy is exposed for all to see. The insecurity and fear are palpable. So, you are constantly trying to cover up, afraid to develop close relationships because you can't afford to let other people get too close. You are deathly afraid that if they do, they will discover the real you and then will reject you. Deep down, you feel desperately wrong, broken, fundamentally flawed and damaged beyond repair. So, you conceal yourself and put on a mask, or false image that you show the world. However, masks can't stay on forever, so you self-isolate, and hide in plain sight with "low hanging fruit" people who don't challenge you.

Lack of self-acceptance will keep you from building supportive relationships and leads to tremendous personal and inter-personal conflict, trauma and anxiety. Self-acceptance is supreme self-validation. It is the personal acknowledgement that you are somebody unique, special and acceptable. It is a precondition to loving or even liking yourself. Failure to accept yourself will often lead to you discounting yourself, and entering or staying in a bad job, relationship, or friendship, because you think you don't deserve better, or that nobody would want you if they really knew you. People who do not accept themselves end up living way beneath God's plan and purpose for their lives.

This leads to a crucial point. Lack of self-acceptance is really an affront to God. It is like giving God a poor grade on His performance review! He didn't do a good job in creating you. He was asleep on the job and let a defective, flawed, specimen of humanity go past in the assembly line. People who don't accept themselves have a hard time believing that anyone else, including God, can accept or love them. So, they doubt and question God's love, or set about to earn His approval through their own performance, works of the flesh, or exacting service. Because we are made in God's image, lack of self-acceptance warps and obscures our view of God. This is because, when you don't see yourself correctly, you won't see God correctly.

Lack of self-acceptance manifests itself in self-criticism, negative self-talk, self-deprecation, low self-esteem, and punishing oneself with negative thoughts and actions. Think about it! You are with you one hundred percent of the time. You can never get away from you. So, if you don't accept yourself, you will feel bad all the time and be unhappy no matter where you are, or what you are doing. It may manifest as jealousy, envy, anger, insecurity, or depression, but it's all rooted in this one thing, self-lack and feeling like you are not enough.

> *You are critical to the plan of God on planet earth.*

Self-acceptance enables you to live life with a sense of wellbeing, health, peace and empowerment. It makes you humble, resilient, and strong; increases your motivation, and supports better physical and emotional health. Self-acceptance provides the foundation for meaningful long term relationships.

Also, self-acceptance helps you to care for yourself, the real you, and positions you to care for others with true compassion. It empowers you to be confident in your own looks, opinions, abilities, interests, and beliefs. It enables you to be comfortable in your own skin. Self-acceptance supports personal autonomy, independence and sound decision making. It also releases you from the need to control other people or life outcomes. It makes you content with being you. Like Eugene Peterson said in the Message Bible, "You are blessed when you are content with just who you are—no more, no less. That's the moment you find yourselves proud owners of everything that can't be bought" (Matthew 5:5).

> *Self-acceptance is your ability to embrace the whole you, good, bad, and ugly, and be comfortable in that embrace.*

Someone has said that the greatest challenge in life is discovering who you are; the second is being happy with what you find. Like Anthony Gignac, so many people are not happy with who they are, so they make up elaborate disguises and hide-aways, or try to become someone else. But alas, trying to be someone else whether criminally or innocently is doomed to failure. Only you can be you.

You Are Irreplaceable

"It's a Wonderful Life" is a 1946 movie that captivated the world of its time, and is still a Christmas staple for many families even today. It tells the story of George Bailey, a good guy who was severely discouraged at Christmastime. He had so many problems, felt that his life was not beneficial to anyone, and contemplated suicide. In a plot twist, he ends up rescuing his guardian angel, Clarence, who then shows George what his town and family would have been like if he hadn't been born. George saw how his life and presence in the world had made such a massive difference in the lives of so many people. He saw that the world was so much better because of him. That knowledge gave him new meaning and reignited his passion for and appreciation of life.

It's the same with you. Your "mere" presence does make a difference in the world! So, however broken, flawed or useless you feel at the moment, the truth is that you have tremendous worth and value; your life has already left an indelible mark on planet earth; your absence will leave a gaping void that nobody else can fill; people in your future will experience irreparable loss if you are not there; and you will be sorely missed. You are irreplaceable!

I once heard a pastor talk about the difference one person can make even in a large congregation. He said that when you are not at church on any Sunday:

1. There's one less voice singing God's praises.
2. One less prayer being offered.
3. One less person available to meet the need of hurting Christians.
4. One less spiritual gift being exercised to edify the body of Christ, and
5. One less believer present to hear the vital instruction of the word of God that will impact the world.

Never underestimate the power of one person, YOU, to make an extraordinary impact in the world. If you think this is an overstatement, consider the story of Edward Kimball. He was a carpet salesman in Boston. He taught a Sunday school class of high school boys at the Mount Vernon Congregational Church. He was concerned about an 18 year old boy in his class who wasn't yet a Christian. Edward prayed for him regularly, but decided he ought to do more than pray. He needed to share the gospel with him. So, he went to the boy's workplace, the Houghton shoe store in Boston. He walked up and down the sidewalk in front of the store for a few minutes to gather the courage to go in. Finally, he went in and asked the boy whether he could talk to him, the boy said yes, and together they went into the stock room, and Edward shared the gospel with him. The young boy gave his life to Christ, his name was Dwight Lyman Moody. D.L. Moody became the greatest evangelist of the 19th century. He led multitudes to Christ, started the Moody Bible Institute, and wrote books and sermons that are still blessing the world today. He preached evangelistic crusades all over America, and led another man to Christ named J Wilber Chapman. Chapman became a Presbyterian minister and evangelist. Because of his ministry, an ex-baseball player named Billy Sunday came to Christ. Billy traveled the country preaching evangelistic crusades in the late 19th and early 20th centuries and led many to Christ. In 1924, Billy went to Charlotte North Carolina for a crusade. Many people were led to the Lord, and there was such a revival in the city that a new organization of business men, the Charlotte Christian Business Men's club was formed. Ten years later, in 1934, they sponsored an evangelistic crusade and invited another well-known minister named Mordecai Ham to lead the crusade. One night, after his message, Mordecai Ham gave an altar call, and down the sawdust aisle walked another young man named Billy Graham who gave his life to Christ that night. Billy Graham became a worldwide evangelist who preached to more unbelievers around the world than any other human being.

Like Edward Kimball, you can make an extraordinary impact on the world. You may feel unqualified, uneducated, untrained, under-gifted or even unworthy. Yet those are excellent qualifications for

God to do a mighty work (Chuck Swindoll). This is because God chooses the unqualified! He chooses those whom the world considers foolish to shame those who think they are wise, and He chooses the puny and powerless to shame the high and mighty. He chooses the lowly, the laughable in the world's eyes, the nobodies, to shame the somebodies. He chooses what is regarded as insignificant to supersede the prominent, so that nobody can boast in His presence.

> *Self-acceptance is supreme self-validation.*

Here's the sum. You are critical to the plan of God on planet earth. There is only one of you in the universe and you are it! You have the one thing that nobody else has – YOU - your voice, your mind, your story, your vision, your history, and yes, even your pain and mistakes. You are the only person qualified to be you, and to fulfill your destiny on planet earth. In fact, right now, someone, somewhere, is depending on you to do what God has created and called you to do. So, be yourself. Talk, and laugh, and sing, and smile, and build, and write, and play and dance and live as only you can. The world is so much better because of you!

CHAPTER 3
YOUR IDENTITY

Your identity is who you are at your core, the way you see, perceive or think about yourself; the way you present yourself to the world, and the characteristics that define you. It is the sum total of all the qualities, beliefs, personality traits and individual markers that identify and distinguish you as a unique person. Your identity is how you define yourself. It includes the unique combination of individual internal, external, physical, intellectual, family, emotional, and spiritual components, convictions, and belief systems that make you, you; and form your sense of self.

A key component of your identity is your name. It is at once a statement of fact, declaration and prophetic utterance. It connects you with your heritage and sometimes with the religion, hopes, beliefs, expectations, aspirations and affirmation of your parents. Other key components of identity include your self-image (your internal model of yourself), your temperament, core values, personality, strengths and weaknesses. In addition, a person's identity is also molded and shaped by factors such as nationality, race, ethnicity, physical appearance, culture, talents, interest, language, and religion.

Identity formation begins early in life. It starts with the initial, fledgling, self-awareness, around three to five years of age, when we realize that we are individuals, distinct and different from our mom, siblings and other family members. Identity is typically acquired from one's parents and family originally; and then framed, sculpted and validated by individual experiences, social interactions, and inter-personal relationships, as well as interface with teachers, authority figures, friends, and role models. It is later reinforced, affirmed, and confirmed by our choices, allegiances, predisposition, associations, and thought process.

Children tend to define themselves through, and draw their self-esteem from, the eyes, speech, attention and affirmation of the authority figures in their lives. If their parents look at them with exasperation, demean them, and speak to or treat them as a nuisance, they will define themselves as worthless and a nobody. If their teachers tell them that they are not smart and cannot achieve, they believe them and set about to fulfill that prediction.

But as they grow, they can recapture and reconnect with their innate potential, and redefine themselves through development of their own independent beliefs, values and skills that differ from and supplant what their parents ingrained in them. This definition has in some cases been so dramatic that the child changes their names and physical appearance to align with their new found identity. Sometimes, further along, another authority figure enters their lives, like a coach or another teacher or mentor at church, who sees them differently and speaks to the latent abilities within them. These new voices clear out the cobwebs of the past, dislodge the wrong thinking, awaken in them a desire to see themselves through a different lens, calls them to greatness, and challenges them to redefine themselves in a way that defeats the negative stereotypes from their past.

> *Whatever your identity, that is what you are empowered to become.*

A critical influence that can upend our existing self-definition and lead to a dramatic redefinition of ourselves, is an encounter with Almighty God. His voice can untangle the web of our past and forge a new future. The Bible provides several examples of how the voice of God broke through longstanding negative or limiting identities and precipitated a foundational change that provoked a new identity, allowed the individual to become a brand new person, and achieve what was previously inconceivable to them.

Abram and Sarai were a regular middle eastern couple living a normal family life in Ur of the Chaldeans, when the voice of God broke into their lives and God said to Abram, "Leave your native country, your relatives, and your father's family, and go to the land that I will show you. I will make you into a great nation" (Genesis 12:1-2). Abram obeyed! He was seventy five years old when God first spoke to him. At ninety nine years old, God made a covenant with him and said: "I will make you the father of a multitude of nations! What's more, I am changing your name. It will no longer be Abram. Instead, you will be called Abraham, for you will be the father of many nations" (Genesis 17:4-5). God changed his name from Abram, which means "exalted father", to Abraham, which means, "Father of many". That name change was a reflection and confirmation of a major self-redefinition that was absolutely critical not only to Abraham's future, but to the future of the entire world. God also changed the name of his wife from Sarai, which means "princess", to Sarah, which also means princess, but by God's word, additionally denotes "mother of nations" because "kings of nations will be among her descendants". True to their new names and God's promise, Abraham and Sarah did have a son, Isaac, when Abraham was a hundred years old and Sarah was ninety years old.

Abraham's grandson, Jacob was a deceiver, conniver and cheat, just as his name prophesied. He "traded" his brother, Esau, a bowl of beans for Esau's birthright as the first born son, deceived his father into giving him the blessing of the first born, and was an all-around trickster. But on his way back home after decades on the run, Jacob ran right into God. The Bible said that Jacob was all alone and a "man" came and wrestled with him until dawn. "Then the man said, "Let me go, for the dawn is breaking!" But Jacob said, "I will not let you go unless you bless me." "What is your name?" the man asked. He replied, "Jacob." "Your name will no longer be Jacob," the man told him. "From now on you will be called Israel because you have fought with God and with men and have won" (Genesis 32:22-32).

This name change was a destiny moment! Jacob the trickster is transformed by the voice of God into Israel, the prince. The name given to him by that "man" who is really a pre-incarnate manifestation of Christ, is the name of the nation of Israel today! The voice of God broke through a lifetime of shady practices to enact a dramatic self-redefinition that forged a brand new destiny.

Saul was an ardent Pharisee of impeccable pedigree. By his own account, he was, "circumcised the eighth day, of the stock of Israel, of the tribe of Benjamin, a Hebrew of the Hebrews; concerning the law, a Pharisee; concerning zeal, persecuting the church; concerning the righteousness which is in the law, blameless" (Philippians 3:5-6). But on the road to Damascus, he came face to face with the risen Christ, who said to him, "Arise and go into the city, and you will be told what you must do." The same voice spoke concerning Saul, "he is a chosen vessel of Mine to bear My name before Gentiles, kings, and the children of Israel. For I will show him how many things he must suffer for My name's sake" (Acts 9:1-15). The power of the voice of God forced a self-redefinition and Saul, the persecutor of the church, the insolent, blasphemer, and chief of sinners, became apostle Paul, the man who did more to spread the gospel of Jesus Christ around the world than any other apostle. That is the power of God's voice. It causes us to see ourselves through His eyes, and births a self-redefinition that transforms us into that same image.

God is still in the business of dramatically changing the identities of people! Earlier today, I received a text from a man of God who wrote, "Today I celebrate two years of sobriety by the grace of God. Thank God that on the night of October 23rd, 2018, when I was at my lowest and cried out to him, he delivered me from alcoholism, drug use, softened my heart and has put me on the path for eternal life! I will serve him until I see him." That is the power of Almighty God to execute a spectacular shift in a person's heart, transform the landscape of their life, reconstruct their outcomes to victory, and birth in them the plans and purpose of God.

Whatever negative identity, labels, curses, or limitations had been placed or spoken over you in the past, whatever you had believed about yourself that is contrary to the word of God, whatever chains had bound you and held you captive, however long you have been in the mud pit, God is able and ready to break the chains and set you free today! He is able and ready to change your identity from alcoholic to preacher, from drug addict to prayer minister, from fraudster to prince, from barren to father of many nations, and from murderer to apostle! God is still in the business of changing lives, identities, names and destinies, even today!

> *When you know your identity, you are secure in the affirmation of your heavenly father and can be and do all that He created and called you to be and do.*

Empowered to Become

Your identity is of critical importance, because whatever your identity, that is what you are empowered to become. Each of us has a picture in our minds of ourselves, our family, future, and so on. The picture you allow in your mind will determine how you "see" yourself, and that in turn will become a self-fulfilling prophesy and foretell what kind of life you will live.

How you identify yourself will determine your "tribe"; the places, people and things that give you a sense of belonging; where you feel connected, affirmed and loved; what gives you a sense of value; and what outlines your framework of what is possible. Your identity outlines your concept of acceptance; powers your assessment of your own capabilities; constructs your definition of "other"; sets the parameters for your dominant thought processes, shapes your perception of success and failure, and frames your view of the world and your place and role in it.

First Samuel 17 tells the very popular story of David and Goliath. The multi-million dollar question is, "Why in the world did David, a young lad, inexperienced in warfare, kill Goliath, a giant, who is a professional soldier and warrior?" Well, the simple answer is that he believed that he could, and rejected every voice that told him he couldn't! So much so, that when all the trained men of war ran away from Goliath, scared, David ran forward toward him, sling shot in hand. As far as David was concerned, Goliath was as good as dead. But why? Why would young David believe that he could kill Goliath? Well, because of how he defined himself and how he defined Goliath.

Unlike Saul and the other men in the Israelite army, David defined Goliath, not by his physical characteristics as a giant, or his impeccable military credentials and famed battlefield prowess. If he had done that, he would have been grossly outmatched and intimidated like the other men were. Rather, he defined Goliath on the basis of covenant. He called him, "an uncircumcised philistine" and a person who had "defied the army of the living God". At that moment, the fight was fixed and Goliath was facing off, not against young, inexperienced David, but against Almighty God, the creator of the universe. David redefined Goliath and by so doing, reduced him to size. The other men saw themselves fighting Goliath, but

David saw God fighting Goliath. In 1 Samuel 17:45-47 he said:

> You come to me with sword, spear, and javelin, but I come to you in the name of the LORD of Heaven's Armies—the God of the armies of Israel, whom you have defied. Today the LORD will conquer you, and I will kill you and cut off your head. And then I will give the dead bodies of your men to the birds and wild animals, and the whole world will know that there is a God in Israel! And everyone assembled here will know that the LORD rescues his people, but not with sword and spear. This is the LORD's battle, and he will give you to us!

David's identity was not in his military training and skills – he had none! His identity and confidence were solely in his intimate relationship with Jehovah and personal experiences of God's victory in the past. In these three verses, he mentioned the Lord eight times! He had a covenant relationship with God and Goliath did not. Defined this way, there was only one possible outcome for this face off, Goliath will lose.

> *Many times, what we know in our heads contend with the word of God in our hearts, and we defeat ourselves without the enemy ever firing a shot.*

Often times, this is where we lose the battle, in our heads. So many times, what we know in our heads contend with the word of God in our hearts, and we defeat ourselves without the enemy ever firing a shot. This is what happened to the other trained military men of Israel. Their training and experience, which usually was an advantage, turned against them when Goliath changed the rules. Normally, in military campaigns like the one that unfolded in the valley of Elah that day, the opposing armies would face off against each other and begin to fight. The Israelite army was ready for that. They were trained and equipped for that kind of war. But this time was different. As they looked on, Goliath emerged from the Philistine camp and changed the rules right before their eyes. He said in essence, this is a different kind of war. No need for everyone to fight. Let's have a one on one combat. I am a Philistine, give me one man from Israel and let's fight man to man. If I defeat him, we win, but if he defeats me, then you win. His proposal sounds fair and equitable. The only problem is, this man was a giant. He was nine feet tall! The Bible said his bronze coat of mail weighed 125 pounds, and the shaft of his spear was as heavy as a weaver's beam (1 Samuel 17:4).

The Israelites were taken aback. They were used to fighting as a group, but Goliath's proposal is different. Under this new paradigm:
1. One man was basically committing suicide
2. One man bore the weight of defeat or victory for the entire nation – a grave responsibility
3. This made the Israelite army to focus on themselves, individually, and when they did, their personal insecurities and inadequacies came into sharp focus.

You see, even though it sounded fair, Goliath didn't fight fair! He was bigger than all of the men. The Bible states that Saul was the tallest man in Israel and the obvious challenger. In 1 Samuel 9:2, we read that Saul was head and shoulders taller than everyone else. But Goliath was too much, even for him. Saul was tall, but he was not a giant. He was not nine feet tall. He was not like Goliath. And if Saul wouldn't fight him, no one else would.

The problem with a new type of war, or when the unexpected happens, is that we don't know how to react. Because it is new, we have no experience or prior frame of reference. So, we feel inadequate, unprepared, and unqualified to address it. We lose our confidence, lose our nerve, and give in to fear. This is a targeted attack and a favorite strategy of the enemy. That is what happened to the Israelite army. They lost their nerve and fell into fear. Keep in mind that these are not wimpy men – these are seasoned men of war, but a new kind of war makes wimps out of brave men.

This story illustrates how your self-definition is a game changer! The men of war defined themselves as just that, men of war! Even though they had the same Abrahamic covenant as David, they were not used to looking through the lens of covenant in a battlefield. In the theatre of war, they were accustomed to looking through the lens of training and experience. So, that was their singular self-definition in this type of environment. However, the thing about prior experience is that it can handicap you and leave you ill-prepared to handle brand new scenarios. When the unexpected happens, you have to scramble to find a replacement lens through which to view and interpret your circumstances, quickly refocus, develop a new strategy and implement a new solution that is adapted to the situation at hand. Unfortunately, this takes time, and that gap in time, between when you realize, with dismay, that your prior experience is impotent in this new scenario, and when you develop a new game plan, is an open door where the enemy can slither in, breathe fear, press the panic button, and exploit the situation to steal, kill, and destroy.

On October 29, 2018, Lion Air Flight 610, a scheduled domestic flight operated by the Indonesian airline, Lion Air, from Soekarno-Hatta International Airport in Jakarta, to Depati Amir Airport in Pangkal Pinang, crashed into the Java Sea thirteen minutes after takeoff, killing all 189 passengers and crew. It was the first major accident involving the new Boeing 737 MAX series of aircraft, introduced in 2017, and the deadliest involving the Boeing 737 series. The October 2019 final report says that MCAS or Maneuvering Characteristics Augmentation System was the primary cause of the crash. "A faulty sensor, inadequate maintenance, poor pilot training and a failure to heed previous problems with the same aircraft were all contributing factors." MCAS was a new software installed by Boeing in the 737 MAX series. The system automatically pitches the nose of the plane down to prevent the aircraft from entering a stall. Boeing did not inform the airline about this new software, and crews were not informed about MCAS in their training modules for the new jet. The pilot and co-pilot of the aircraft were very experienced. The pilot had over 6000 flight hours and the co-pilot had over 5100 flight hours. But their prior experience did not help them with this new design software.

The flight voice recorder, recovered after the crash, revealed the desperate last minutes of flight 610, in which these experienced pilots searched frantically through the plane's flight manual for how to disable the MCAS, all to no avail. They were not trained for the

MCAS, and so their prior experience failed to aid them in the face of this new software and the unexpected persistent nose dive of the plane. Their anguished search for a way to save themselves and their passengers was heart wrenching, but fruitless. The plane crashed into the sea and killed everyone on board.

This tragic story illustrates the point that while experience is important and a great asset in known situations, it can leave you completely unprepared for new or different circumstances.

For David, his lack of military training and experience became a blessing in disguise. This was a new kind of war and prior military training was not directly applicable, and became in fact a handicap. Besides, due to his lack of experience, David did not fully comprehend how much more qualified Goliath was militarily, and that ignorance relieved him of paralyzing fear. All he knew was how much more powerful his God was! Also, what he lacked in formal military training, he made up for with his experience in unconventional warfare. He had battled a bear and a lion alone in the wilderness, and won. That unconventional experience came in handy. It was exactly what was needed for the one on one kind of battle that Goliath proposed.

David identified himself with God and His covenant, and that qualified him to execute God's judgement on Goliath, as the enemy of God. His self-definition empowered him to win! You see David saw and heard the same things as the Israelite army, but he interpreted it differently because he had a different self-definition and identity. Herein lies the difference:

    1. The Israelite army saw a giant, but David saw an uncircumcised Philistine.

    2. The Israelite army saw their own ability or inability – David saw God's power.

    3. The Israelite army saw themselves dead, David saw Goliath dead!

    4. The Israelite army reacted in fear, David responded with faith.

It is important to note that nobody else saw or defined David the way he defined himself, and so, they did not believe that he could win; in fact, they were convinced that he was headed for certain death. His brother Eliab demeaned him, and tried to "put him in his place" by asking "What are you doing around here anyway? What about those few sheep you're supposed to be taking care of? I know about your pride and deceit. You just want to see the battle!" Never mind that there was no battle to see because Eliab and all the "men of war" were too scared to fight! Saul the king did not believe David could win. When David offered to go and fight Goliath, Saul said, "Don't be ridiculous. There's no way you can fight this Philistine and possibly win. You're only a boy, and he's been a man of war since his youth". Goliath himself did not believe that David was a credible threat! He laughed his head off and said with a sneer, "Am I a dog that you come at me with a stick?" Well, the joke was on him as his severed head ended up in David's hand.

Nobody believed David could win, nobody, but David. And he believed that he could win because he defined himself by and identified himself with his God, and that identity literally catapulted him to victory.

Self-Definition

> *How you see yourself will determine what you can allow yourself to do or become.*

I heard the story of a pig and a sheep that fell into a mud hole. The pig was ecstatic! It lay in the mud, grunted happily, rolled around and had a ball. The mud pit felt like home and the pig was as happy as can be. The sheep on the other hand, was in trouble. It instinctively knew that it did not belong in the mud hole. It did not wallow, or lay down in the mud. It kept trying to get out, even though it would slip and fall back in. But it was adamant, bleating as loudly and as desperately as it could, calling frantically for help to get out of the mud pit. The sheep did not identify with the mud pit. It did not belong there, and instinctively knew that if it stayed in the mud pit, it would die.

This is the same with us. How we see ourselves determines what we can allow ourselves to do or become. If you see yourself as a dirty pig or wearing muddy clothes, it is so much easier to get in the mud pit and wallow. But if you see yourself as wearing a spotless white suit, you would stay far away from the mud hole. This is why identity is so critical, and why the devil works so hard to convince us to adopt the wrong identity. He wants us to put off our God-given, white robe of righteousness and put on the dirty overalls of sin, guilt and condemnation so we can get into the mud pit and settle.

The devil wants you to believe that you are a sinner and utterly powerless against sin, because he knows that, if you see yourself as a dirty sinner, and sin as inevitable, you will give up and wallow in the mud pit like the pig. But the Bible says that God has put on us a spotless white robe of righteousness. To get into the mud pit and stay there, we have to take off our white robe of righteousness! How? In and by our thinking. In our minds, we have to see ourselves in muddy overalls and think of ourselves as powerless, incurable, sinners. Sadly, some churches present this garbage as "humility" and truth, and in so doing assist the devil in his evil work of keeping men and women in bondage.

> *Put off the old and put on the new. It's that simple!*

God on the other hand is quite explicit in the opposite direction. He lets us know that we have the power to cast off our old nature and past behaviors like tattered, muddy overalls, and put on our new nature which is created in righteousness and true holiness. Put off the old and put on the new. It's that simple! He says, "throw off your old sinful nature and your former way of life, which is corrupted by lust and deception. Let the Spirit renew your thoughts and attitudes. Put on your new nature, created to be like God—truly righteous and holy." He then breaks it down into specifics; stop telling lies, rather, speak the truth; don't let anger control you, because it gives a foothold to the devil; if you are a thief, quit stealing. Instead, use your hands for good hard work, and don't use foul or abusive language, instead, let everything you say be good and helpful. (Ephesians 4:22-29).

> *The devil will try to convince you that you are still bound by the things that God has set you free from. Don't believe him!*

When you know your identity, you are secure in the affirmation of your heavenly father and can be and do all that he created and called you to be and do. But if you don't know your identity, the devil will rob you of your inheritance. He will try to deceive you, the sheep, into thinking that you are the pig, and that the mud pit is your natural habitat. He will encourage you to live like the pig, knowing fully well that a life in the mud pit is contrary to your nature and will ultimately kill you. He will try hard to convince you that you are still bound by the things that God has set you free from. Don't believe him!

CHAPTER 4
THE IDENTITY PARABLE

In Luke 15, Jesus tells a parable that has become known as the parable of the prodigal son. The setting is a Middle Eastern family with a wealthy father, two sons and many servants. In this culture, age is revered and family is valued above the individual. The first son has a prized position in the family pecking order. He gets twice the inheritance of his other siblings. The father is the patriarch and commands unquestioning obedience. So, what happens in this story, is truly scandalous!

The second son said to his father, "I want my share of your estate now before you die." How shocking! Normally, the inheritance passes upon the death of the father, but here, this son wants to accelerate the process, and act as if his father was already dead. This was a slap in his father's face. But, this young man knew his identity as a son, laid claim to it and placed a demand on his father. He said, I want "my" share of your estate. That is a sonship declaration. Wrong timing, selfish approach, but nonetheless, his brash request was rooted in an understanding of his identity as a son to his wealthy father.

> *Positive self-talk can empower you to overcome mammoth obstacles and achieve incredible victories.*

In making this request, this young man exalted the individual, himself, above the family, which is taboo. What is even more surprising is that his father agreed. In the culture in which this parable is set, children can be stoned to death for being rebellious and disobedient to their parents (Deuteronomy 21:18-21). But his father did not raise an objection. He knew that misguided as it is, his son was making a valid claim. He was indeed his son, and entitled to a share of the inheritance as his birthright.

Then this son did the unthinkable! He packed up and left his family. First, he disrespected his father, and now he has disrespected his family. In a culture that exalts the family over the individual, he had committed a cardinal sin. He had abandoned his family!

He proceeded to squander his inheritance. When his money ran out, he resorted to self-help methods to keep himself afloat. The Bible said that he began to starve. His starvation was physical, but more than that, he starved of his true identity. He was now in a spot, space, and situation in life that denied, questioned, and repudiated his identity. This was a critical juncture, a fork in the road where he would either reclaim and assert his identity and arise, or denounce his identity and remain in captivity and decline. It's the same crucial juncture we face in every temptation.

His self-help approach appeared to work, at first. He made progress, he got a job, but it was a job that drove him further down the path of potentially losing his identity altogether. For a Jewish boy, feeding pigs is rock bottom! It doesn't get worse than that, or does it? In his case, it did. He not only fed pigs, but he was so low and so famished that he began to desire the putrid mush that the pigs ate! From the penthouse to the garbage dump. That's how low he came. A battle was raging inside of him that eventually spilled out through his lips. A battle of two worlds, two kingdoms, two identities. A battle between pride and humility, rebellion and repentance, dereliction and destiny - the ultimate battle of good and evil.

The hunger within him was not just a hunger for food, it was a hunger for who he was, a hunger to resolve the dichotomy between where he was and who he is; how he looked and who he is; what he did, and who he is. One side of the scale was stacked, with how he looked, where he was, and what he did - his circumstances. And on the other side was just one item, who he was - his identity. That one item outweighed all the others, but it required courage, humility, faith, and genuine repentance for him to walk in it.

I like the way the King James Version of the Bible describes what happened next. It says that he "came to himself". This implies that the actions he had taken previously, asking for his inheritance, leaving his family, moving to another land, living wildly, and working in the pig farm, represented a departure from himself. Those actions were not consistent with who he was. They represented a disconnection from his true identity and core purpose. They were an aberration. He thought he was living "the life", but instead, he was destroying himself.

What was the thought process that brought him back to himself? What train of thought overrode the feeling of condemnation, guilt, shame, pride, and reproach, to allow him to reconnect with his true self? Did he remember his early years when his father talked to him and his brother about what it meant to be a man, their family legacy, his Jewish heritage, the covenants with God, and the faith and obedience of Abraham? The Bible doesn't tell us the litany of thoughts that ran through his mind, but it does tell us about his self-talk. He said to himself:

"At home, even the hired servants have food enough to spare, and here I am dying of hunger! I will go home to my father and say, "Father, I have sinned against both heaven and you, and I am no longer worthy of being called your son. Please take me on as a hired servant." (Luke 15: 17-19).

> *When you give voice to your self-talk, it is a game changer!*

"Self-talk" is the endless stream of unspoken thoughts that run through your head. It outlines the image of yourself that you have on the inside. If these thoughts are mostly negative, then your outlook on life is likely to be pessimistic, but, if they are positive, your outlook on life will be bright and optimistic. Self-talk is what you say about yourself, to yourself. Positive self-talk can empower you to overcome mammoth obstacles and achieve incredible victories. But negative self-talk can disempower you and reduce you to a whimpering, spineless, wimp; incapable of making the simplest decisions. When you give voice to your self-talk, it is a game changer!

Matthew 19:20-22 illustrates the immense power of self-talk to unlock victory in the life of a believer. It tells how a nameless woman deliberately drew healing power from Jesus without His express consent. She initiated, scheduled, activated, and obtained her miracle by her faith-filled words. She kept saying to herself, "If I only touch His outer robe, I will be healed." Well, she did, and she was. Jesus said to her, "Daughter, be encouraged! Your faith has made you well." And she was healed at that moment.

For the second son in Luke 15, his thoughts took him from his present location in the pig pen, to a place in his mind called "home". In his mind's eye, he saw his father's house and the abundant lifestyle he had enjoyed at "home". He then contrasted it with "here" and there was a significant gap. "Here" has eventually become the pig pen, but not at first. "Here" had looked so attractive when he was home. "Here" had made alluring promises of fun, excitement, pleasure and fulfillment, when he was "home". But, as often happens, "here" has failed to deliver on its promise. The dream had turned into a nightmare and he now realized what his father had known all along, that sin makes promises that it cannot keep. He learned that there is no place like home and that "here" can never be a match for "Home". His desire and lust for "here" had brought him to this low and desperate place where the hired servants in his father's house were much better off that he was. His lust for "here" has led him to the pig pen!

His gap analysis was spot on! But what he did next was the most important thing. He decided to exercise his will! So many people come to the same place that he did, the place where they admit that sin has not kept its promises, and that the Father's house is far better that the "far country", but alas, they fall short of making a decision. So many people are just one decision away from reclaiming their identity. The second son said, "I WILL". Those are the key words that determine the pivot points in our lives, the destiny moments when we transition from analysis and thought, to personal responsibility, accountability, and action. He said, "I will arise and go home to my father" and he did. But before he did, he comes up with a plan that gives us an insight into his state of mind. He wrote his homecoming speech. He started off right, "Father I have sinned against both heaven and you". That is really all he needed to say. Did you notice how he did not just focus on heaven? This is an important note, that forgiveness is not just vertical, but is horizontal as well. When we have sinned against God and people, it is necessary to ask forgiveness of both parties, and make restitution as needed.

But then he continued to say, "I am no longer worthy of being called your son. Please take me on as a hired servant." This time, he missed it by a mile! His heart was in the right place but his thoughts, plans, and self-help approach took him to the wrong conclusion. He was his father's son. He didn't do anything to deserve that, and he can't do anything to undo that. There will never be a minute in his entire life and in eternity, when he will not be the biological son of his father. His father may disown him, but he cannot change his DNA. He is his father's son forever! He carries his father's DNA. His sonship was not a status that can be changed at will, it was his heritage. It was unchangeable! It does not depend on his worth or lack thereof. It is not an achievement to be earned or lost. Even if his father had agreed to his request and taken him as a hired servant, he would still be a son, but a son who is living as a hired servant.

> *Sin, guilt, shame, and condemnation cannot undo your sonship or change who you are in Christ.*

This speech is so reminiscent of the false humility that has afflicted many in the body of Christ. "Take me on as a hired servant" sounded very humble, but it was the voice of the enemy and the flesh. It was the voice of guilt, condemnation, legalism, and religion. It was the devil's strategy to hold him in bondage. He couldn't simply ask his father for forgiveness. He thought he had to work for it. It's as if his unearned forgiveness, freely given and freely received, will bankrupt heaven! Today, the devil is still holding many in bondage with that same thought process, wanting to make them pay for what Jesus has already paid for in full; saying in essence, that Jesus's sacrifice is not enough.

Your sin, guilt, shame, and condemnation cannot undo your sonship or change who you are in Christ. It will open the door to the devil and give him an inroad into your life, but it will not change your standing before God. You are a child of God, and that is an eternal truth. In John 10:28, Jesus said that He gives us eternal life, and we shall never perish, and nobody can pluck us out of His hand.

Notice that the second son was his father's son when he was at home, when he left for the far country, and when he was in the pig pen. His circumstances changed, but his sonship did not. His self-centeredness, sin, rebellion, wild living and pig-farm job did not strip him of his identity. He was no less a son of his father in anyone of those situations, than on the day he came home and was restored, cleaned and clothed. He was still the same on the inside. All he needed to do was to "come to himself", reclaim his identity and walk in it. When he did, he found out that his father still loved him just the same. Regardless of how he looked, felt and smelled, he was still his father's son! His identity was irrevocable! While he was focused on giving his planned speech, his father was focused on receiving, blessing and restoring him.

> *Four things we lose when we don't know our identity in Christ – our righteousness, authority, dominion, and access to the resources of God.*

His father saw him a long way off and ran to him, which in that culture says a great deal about his father's longing, love and compassion for him. He embraced and kissed him, even though he was dirty, and smelled like the pig sty he came from. His father didn't let him finish his rehearsed apology. He spoke to the servants, "Quick! Bring the finest robe in the house and put it on him. Get a ring for his finger and sandals for his feet. And kill the calf we have been fattening. We must celebrate with a feast, for this son of mine was dead and has now returned to life. He was lost, but now he is found" (Verses 22-24). Notice that he called him, "son of mine". He restored him fully and completely:

1. He gave him the finest robe – righteousness and right standing
2. Put a ring on his finger – authority
3. Sandals for his feet – dominion
4. Killed the fatted calf – abundance and prosperity

The father did not hold back anything! He did not reprimand him, wait for him to "work out" his repentance or earn his way back into his father's good graces. He did not shun or humiliate him, recount his evil ways, or point a finger at him and say, "I told you so". He did not say "you have squandered your inheritance, so there's no more inheritance left for you". No! He received him just as he was, cleaned him up and restored him.

Notice that the items restored by his father, righteousness, authority, dominion and abundance are the very things that the enemy robbed him of, and these are the same things the enemy tries to steal from us when we don't know our identity in Christ.

Four Things We Lose When We Don't Know Our Identity in Christ

1. Robe of righteousness – Our righteousness and right standing with God.

2. Ring – our authority as believers

3. Sandals – our dominion and rule in the earth

4. Abundance – our access to the resources of God.

Our heavenly Father wants to restore all these and more to us.

The Miracle of Restored Identity

What Jesus wants us to see in the life of this young man is the miracle of restored identity. We call him "the prodigal son", but that is not what his father called him. He called him, "son of mine". That was the key to his restoration. This young man had been known by his worst mistake, but that is not how his father saw him. His worst mistake, terrible as it was, did not redefine or change his identity. He was still his father's son! What anybody else called him was irrelevant. All that mattered was what his father called him, and he called him "son".

We see this same miracle in the life of the "woman with the issue of blood". She is not even called by her name. Everybody knew her by her problem. For twelve years, she had been afflicted with this terrible malady that slowly drained the life out of her, consumed her resources, self-worth, and sense of belonging. She was an outcast. When she crawled on her hands and knees to touch Jesus, she saw herself exactly like other people saw her, dirty, filthy, smelly, and a nobody. But Jesus wouldn't let her get away with that mindset and identity. Yes, she was physically healed when she touched Him, but she was still so broken, scarred, and un-whole on the inside. All those years of dehumanization had taken a toll. Jesus needed to find her, look her in the eye, and give her the miracle of a restored identity. So, He scanned the crowd and asked, "who touched me?" Peter protested, "Master, this whole crowd is pressing up against you." How can you say, "who touched me?" But Jesus would not let it go. Finally, when she realized that she could not stay hidden, she fell, trembling, to her knees in front of Him, told Him her whole story and why she touched Him. (Luke 8:43-48).

There and then, in front of that whole crowd, which most likely included people who had ridiculed, rejected and ostracized her, He restored her rightful identity. He called her daughter!

She had been called many obscene and humiliating names. Her most popular name was, "the woman with the issue of blood." It was a no-name, embarrassing label. She had lost all dignity, even the basic dignity of a name! She had a problem that could not be hidden. It was so public and so pervasive that it had become her identity. But Jesus did not call her by that despicable label. He gave her a new identity. He called her daughter! He said to her "Daughter, your faith has made you well. Go in peace." Now her healing was complete! She was healed and made whole not only physically, but in her soul. Jesus healed and restored her emotionally, socially, relationally and mentally. He is still doing this miracle today.

> *Regardless of your past, Jesus wants to give you a new identity - son or daughter of Almighty God.*

So, regardless of who you are or what you've done, your past sins, mistakes or status, Jesus wants to restore you and give you a new identity - son or daughter of Almighty God. John 1:12 says it very eloquently, "But to all who did receive him, he gave them the right to become children of God, to those who believe in his name," All you have to do is to believe and receive Christ.

To receive God's miracle of a restored identity, pray this prayer out loud: "Lord Jesus, I believe in you. Come into my heart. I receive you as my Lord and Savior – Amen."

Welcome to the family of God! You are now a son or daughter of Almighty God. Please connect with a local Bible believing church to learn and grow in Christ. Also, contact me on my website www.gloriagodson.com, or by email so I can rejoice with you and give you some resources to help you in your new walk of faith. My email address is at the back of this book.

CHAPTER 5
MISTAKEN IDENTITY

According to a death certificate, 18-year-old Whitney Cerak died on April 26, 2006. Nearly 1,400 people attended her funeral before she was buried in her hometown of Gaylord, Michigan. But five weeks after the tragic car accident that killed Whitney and four others, a shocking mix-up was revealed. Whitney was not the girl who died that day. In an inconceivable mistake, Whitney had been mistaken for Laura Van Ryn. Both girls and seven others were in a van heading back to Taylor University in Indiana, when they were hit by a semi-truck that lost control and ran into their van.

An official at the scene of the accident found Laura's purse next to Whitney, and put Laura's identification with Whitney, and just like that, Whitney became Laura. At the hospital, Emergency Room doctors were able to stabilize Whitney, who they believed to be Laura. They transferred her to the intensive care unit, and Laura's family was notified of what they believed to be their daughter's status.

While Laura's family raced to the hospital to be by their daughter's side; across town, the county coroner began his grim task. Taylor University staff worked with the coroner's office to identify the deceased. At that point, Laura Van Ryn's body was wrongly identified as Whitney Cerak. Whitney's family did not look at the body to identify it. Whitney's sister, Carly, did not want to see her sister crushed from the accident. At this point, Whitney and Laura's identities were officially switched.

Back at the hospital, Laura's parents, Don and Susie; and her sister, Lisa, are told not to expect Laura to look like herself, because she has been through a horrible accident. When they first saw the girl they believed to be Laura, they could only see part of her face. She had bandages around her head, tubes in her mouth, a tube in her head, and many cuts and bruises.

With no other reason to believe the girl in the hospital wasn't their daughter, the Van Ryns started a vigil with family and friends that lasted for five weeks. They took turns at the hospital so that someone was always by her side. It was not until five weeks later that Whitney said her name, and told Laura's sister, Lisa, that her last name was "Cerak" and her parents were "Newell and Colleen, not Don and Susie."

Needless to say, this colossal fiasco took a severe emotional and human toll on both families, particularly, the Van Ryn's, who had to hold a second funeral service for their daughter, weeks after she was first buried under a different name.

My Name is Whitney!

Whitney Cerak and Laura Van Ryn looked alike. They were both blonde, had fairly the same height and physical features. They looked so alike that they were mistaken for one another for five whole weeks. However, neither their physical similarities, nor the words, sincere belief and confirmations of the coroner, doctors,

Taylor University staff, or even family members could turn Whitney into Laura. Whitney Cerak remained Whitney Cerak regardless of who others thought or said she was. Everybody thought that Whitney was dead, except Whitney.

The doctors called her Laura, the nurses called her Laura, the Van Ryn family called her Laura, but that did not change who she was. She was Whitney, and what everybody else called her did not matter. What mattered was what she called herself. As soon as she could speak, she identified herself and called herself by her name – Whitney.

When she was brought to the hospital, she did not look like Whitney. Her head was covered with bandages, and she had tubes coming out of her head and body. She looked bad, disfigured, and bloodied, but that did not change her identity. She was Whitney Cerak when she was all beautiful and dolled up, and she was Whitney Cerak when she was bloodied and disfigured. Her circumstances did not change who she was. The accident did not change who she was. Her physical appearance did not change who she was. She was Whitney, no matter what!

She lost her voice and could not speak for herself, but that did not change her identity. Everybody called her Laura, but they could not make her become Laura without her consent! The day came when she regained consciousness, her memory, a little strength, and her voice; not all of it, but just a little whisper. That day, for the first time, five weeks into the ordeal, she whispered in a little voice - "my name is Whitney", and that changed everything!

The accident took her voice, her health, and almost her life, but it could not change who she was. She was Whitney Cerak, and nobody could change that! She was pronounced dead, buried in her hometown and a crowd of over 1400 people witnessed it, but that did not kill her. People may have had her funeral, but they had it without her consent!

You Belong to God!

Do you know your name? Do you know who you are? Do you know whose you are?

Like Whitney, people or the devil may try to pin an identity on you that is not yours – don't accept it! They put Laura's pocket book and identity on Whitney, but that did not make Whitney become Laura. She was still who she was. Your identity is set by your heavenly Father! You are who He says that you are and nobody can change that!

> *Your identity is set by your heavenly Father! You are who He says that you are and nobody can change that!*

The Bible says that if you've made Jesus your Lord and savior, then you are a son or daughter of Almighty God. You are an heir of God and a joint-heir with Christ. You have the DNA of God. You are a partaker of his divine nature. You have the mind of Christ. You are a king and priest unto God. You are anointed to prosper and empowered to succeed in all that you lay your hands to do.

You may be beaten, battered, and trampled upon by life, but that does not and cannot change your value or identity. In his book, *25*

Ways to Win with People, John Maxwell provided a vivid illustration. A $100 bill may be crumpled, tossed on the ground, stepped on, and ground into the dust. But it will never lose its value. It is still a $100 bill and legal tender for goods and services regardless of how dirty or crumpled it is. The same analogy is applicable to us as human beings. We may be dropped, crumpled, ground into the dust, and dirtied by life, but that will never devalue us because our value comes from God, our creator, not from our status, circumstances, or the approval or opinion of other people (*Choosing A Life of Victory*).

Don't let sickness, a frightening diagnosis, bankruptcy, divorce, singleness, breakups, fear, or anything else rename you or change who you are. Declare who you are, and whose you are – you are a child of Almighty God! You see, the only ones who had a right to name Whitney were her parents, and the name they called her stuck regardless of the horrendous circumstances that tried to strip her of that name and identity. God is your Father, and He calls you blessed, victorious, healthy, successful, strong, and favored, and nobody can strip you of those names or your identity in God.

The devil may try to define you by your limitation, the opinion of other people or a label. Labels like ex-convict, addict, alcoholic, or homeless. Take those labels off! Refuse the false identity of the devil and accept only your heavenly Father's love, identity and affirmation. The Bible says that nothing can ever separate you from God's love.

> *Fight with words, God's word and your words.*

Today, if you feel like Whitney, battered and bruised by life, or barraged by voices, both well-meaning and hostile; that call you names like loser, failure, lost cause, or under achiever, refuse to accept that identity. Rebel against it in your heart and refuse to be defined by those voices or your present circumstances. Focus on getting better – don't fight with your detractors right now. Don't respond to those who are calling you names right now. Run to God. Let Him heal and restore you. Get well, get better, then fight! Fight with words, God's word and your words. Reclaim your true identity as a child of the Most High God. Say it out of your mouth, "I am a child of the Most High God!" It doesn't matter what has transpired and for how long you have been wrongly characterized, like Whitney, those voices will be drowned and those labels lose their grip at the sound of your voice, proclaiming who you are in Christ.

Today, Whitney is alive and well. What tried to kill her became her pathway to fame. Six years later, she had her wedding in the same church where her funeral had been held. She speaks to you and I not to give up, even when people count you out and mark you as dead and forgotten. That is their opinion. They may have a right to express their opinion, but you have the corresponding right to ignore it. If they are not God, their opinion is irrelevant. Remember, God can change things on a dime, and it's never over until He says so!

God approved of you before anybody else ever had a chance to disapprove. And His approval does not depend on your works, looks, performance, or meeting other people's expectations. Don't worry about other people's opinions of you. God's opinion is the only one that matters and He is crazy about you. You can't make everyone like, love, validate, accept, or be nice to you. You can't control them either, but the good news is, it doesn't matter. Not every person is going to understand, support, or encourage you and that is okay. You have God's approval and that is all you need.

God has selected you, so it doesn't matter who rejects or neglects you. God's favor outweighs all the opposition and positions you to win. Other people may have more talent, education, or experience, but God's favor can cause you to go places you could not go on your own. God will not allow anybody or anything to keep you from your destiny. They may be bigger, stronger and more powerful, but God knows how to get you to where you are supposed to be. Simply refuse to be defined by those negative voices or your present circumstances, and reclaim your true identity as a child of Almighty God.

> *To reclaim your identity, find out what the Bible says about you, believe it as truth, and replace every negative thought and voice with the word of God.*

How can you reclaim your identity? Find out what the Bible says about you, believe it as truth; replace every negative thought and voice with the word of God; and speak the word of God over yourself. Say the same thing about yourself, that God says about you, and you will see the victory of God in every area of your life.

CHAPTER 6
IDENTITY IS FOUNDATIONAL

When I started writing this book, I knew that for a Christian, identity in Christ is pivotal and undergirds all outcomes in life. So, I set about to outline the contours of identity, and the breadth and depth of identity formation in the life of a Christian. This is a topic I am passionate about, so I thought the words would flow easily. But my writing stalled. As I prayed and sought God for clarity and direction on what He wants me to write, He spoke to me very clearly, that I needed to look at this topic with fresh eyes. He said "This is the most important book you've written so far", and He wanted me to approach it with uncommon intensity. I asked why? And He said, "Because, every problem a Christian has is an identity problem; every temptation is an identity challenge; and every sin is an identity crisis issue!" Wow!

> *Every problem a Christian has is an identity problem; every temptation is an identity challenge; and every sin is an identity crisis issue!*

Every Problem is an Identity Problem

God created man in His own image. Before He created man, He created the garden of Eden and provided everything that man would ever need. He created the heavens and the earth; land, air, and sea, and filled them. Then He created man to superintend and rule over all creation, acting in His stead, as god. Man disobeyed God and ceded his authority over creation to the devil. Mankind fell, along with creation and his jurisdiction over it. Then God set out on a rescue mission, to redeem and restore fallen humanity. He set about to establish a spiritual kingdom that is superior to and counter to the kingdom of this world that man had turned over to the enemy. Jesus, the last Adam, came to earth to inaugurate this kingdom. That was his express mission and He made that clear right away. Mark 1:14-15, states: "Jesus came to Galilee, preaching the gospel of the kingdom of God, and saying, "The time is fulfilled, and the kingdom of God is at hand. Repent, and believe in the gospel." Through Christ, God restored to mankind everything that Adam lost and re-established mankind's rule over creation.

However, everything God did was in the spirit realm. In Christ, mankind was recreated anew in the spirit and restored to power and authority. Once again God provided for everything man would need, this provision is in His word. Ephesians 1:3 states that He blessed us with all spiritual blessings in the heavenly realms, and 2 Peter 1:3 confirms that He gave us everything we need for living a godly life. Simply stated, God has made provision for every need mankind will ever have. That provision is in His word. There is no human condition that the Word of God does not address, and there is no problem on earth that the word of God cannot solve.

When a problem emerges in the life of a believer, it is an identity confrontation. The problem is making a demand on your identity. It is essentially asking you the question, "who are you?" In Mark 11:23-24, Jesus taught us to speak to the mountain. This is because your mountain or problem is speaking to you. It is challenging your identity, and asking you in essence to "put up or shut up". How you see your problem is critical. If you see it through the lens of your identity as a child of God, you can go to the word of God, find the provision that God has made for that need, and apply it to your situation to achieve the outcome that God promised. That is how to exercise our God-given authority to overcome. But if you see the problem only through the eyes of your humanity, then you can get into fear, run helter-skelter, have a panic attack, and resort to works of the flesh.

> *In Christ, your identity is that you are a child of God.*

In Christ, your identity is that you are a child of God. You are an heir of God and a joint heir with Christ. You are seated in heavenly places in Christ, you have the DNA of God. You are a partaker of His divine nature. You have the mind of Christ. In Him you live and move and have your being. You are His offspring! As Jesus is, so are you in this world! You are a brand new creation in the spirit, and the Holy Spirit who lives inside you, equips you to fight and empowers you to win in every battle.

A couple weeks ago, a gym song was stuck in my head, a very catchy song with the lyrics, "I'm only human after all, I'm only human after all, don't put your blame on me". It kept playing over and over in my head, and I bobbed my head to the tune. But then, the Holy Spirit nudged me to stop and think about the lyrics. I did, and ended up rebuking the song from my mind! That song may be catchy, but for me as a child of God, it is a lie from the pit of hell. I am NOT only human. The Bible says that I am born of God's Spirit and indwelt by the Holy Spirit. The same Spirit that raised up Jesus from the dead lives in me. So, I AM a supernatural being. I am not only human, or "just" a woman. At least one third of me is wall to wall Holy Spirit, and as I learn to connect with Him, hear Him, live by faith, and operate from the realm of the spirit, my soul space will be wholly filled and flooded with God Himself, come under the Lordship of Christ, and the direction of the Holy Spirit. So, I am growing increasingly more and more supernatural!

> *You are not only human. You are a supernatural being. At least one third of you is wall to wall Holy Spirit.*

When we approach problems from that place of authority and dominion, instead of fear and powerlessness, the outcomes are different every single time. Thinking that we are ONLY human limits our ability to walk in our identity and authority as children of God.

Every Temptation is an Identity Challenge

Hidden in every temptation is the question, "Are you really a child of God, and by how much?" In other words, every temptation is a test to find out what it will take to get you to disavow, renounce, denigrate, and abandon your heritage as a child of God. The temptation is asking, "What will it take to get you to break your allegiance to God and His word, rule, and authority in your life? It is saying to you, "talk is cheap, let's see what you will do under pressure."

We see this macabre drama play out in the book of Job, where the devil essentially said to God, "Job is serving you because of all the goodies you've packed into his life. Take all of it away and he will drop you like a hot potato". You see, this is the age old conflict! The devil lost his position in heaven because he rebelled against God's authority. He has since set about to prove that human beings, if given the chance, would abandon God's rule, just like he did. He wants to justify his sin and rebellion, and he wants to use human beings to prove his point. Every time a Christian abandons God and His word because of persecution, hardship, or problems, they help the devil prove his point, that God is not worthy of worship, just because He is God.

First John 3:7-10, states that we have the nature of God in us and sin is contrary to our nature. Apostle John warns us to watch out for the deceiver, the devil, who will try to beguile us into thinking that our old sinful nature still has control, that sin is still our master, and that we have no choice but to obey the dictates of sin. But the devil is a liar! The power of sin has been broken in our lives. Sin is no longer our master and we do not have to serve it! We are born again by the incorruptible seed of the word of God, which lives and abides forever. The same word that was made flesh in Christ is in us. The same power that raised Jesus from the dead lives inside us.

Whatever temptations we face today follow a predictable pattern. It is a challenge to our identity in Christ. In his first temptation, the devil challenged the identity of the first man and woman. They were made in the image of God, but he told them that if they listened to him, and disobeyed God, then they would become like God. They did not know their identity, and so they were conned by the devil to trade who they were, everything they had, and their relationship with God for something they already had. The devil promised to sell them what God had already freely given to them, and he lured them to get it through pride and disobedience. Essentially, he offered them the option to be like God, without God. Sound familiar? It should. It's the same "New Age" tactic he uses today.

Same thing with Jesus! The devil said to him, "If you are the son of God", again, challenging His identity. But Jesus thoroughly defeated the devil and sent him running with his tail between his legs. He refused to prove anything to the devil. He knew who he was, and that was enough. He would not perform, parade, trade or even pay the devil any mind. Eventually, he told him to get out! And he did.

In 1 Corinthians 10:13, the Bible warns us to beware of Satan's tricks. God assures us that the temptations in our lives are no different from what others experience. And God is faithful. He will not allow the temptation to be more than we can bear in His strength. So, when we are tempted, if we lean on Him, He will show us a way out so that we can endure. This scripture is an antidote to the devil's, "you only" trick. This is the trick he used on Elijah the man of God, and deceived him into thinking that he was the only prophet of Jehovah left, and so, this mighty man of God who called down fire from heaven, ran in suicidal panic from one woman and went and hid in a cave. When God asked him, "what are you doing here Elijah?" He responded with a lie the devil had told him. He said, "the people of Israel have ... killed every one of your prophets. I am the only one left, and now they are trying to kill me, too." God corrected his misinformation. God said to him, "I have reserved seven thousand in Israel, all whose knees have not bowed to Baal, and every mouth that has not kissed him" (1 Kings 19:1-17).

It's the same lie the devil peddles even today. He wants to convince us that our situation is so peculiar, so different, that it would justify our sin or disobedience to God. No one has ever endured such a horrendous trial; so, it's okay if we can't or don't endure it. It's okay if we fail, after all, we are only mere human beings. In fact, it is unjust of God to allow us to go through such unbearable pressure. It's too much and we have a right to put an end to it, and get some relief, right now!

> *Every time a Christian abandons God and His word because of persecution, hardship, or problems, they help the devil prove his point,* **that** *God is not worthy of worship, just because He is God.*

Well, God has already warned us about the devil's strategy. It's an old trick, repackaged with new glossy lure adapted for each person. Apostle John affirms, "For all that *is* in the world—the lust of the flesh, the lust of the eyes, and the pride of life—is not of the Father but is of the world. And the world is passing away, and the lust of it; but he who does the will of God abides forever (1 John 2:16-17). Did you get that? This is ALL that is in the world, nothing more! The devil's entire bag of tricks consists of a craving for physical pleasure, a craving for everything we see, and pride in our achievements and possessions. It's what he tempted the first Adam with and what he tempted the last Adam with. It's what he tempts us with even today. The how is different, but the what is still the same. Be on the alert, and do not fall for the devil's ploy.

Sometimes our misinterpretation of 1 Corinthians 10:13 plays into the devil's strategy. Often, people interpret that scripture to mean that God will not allow you to be tempted with something that you can't handle or are not ready for. For example, "God won't allow me to be tempted with adultery because He knows I can't handle it." But that interpretation is flawed. Apostle Paul himself, who wrote 1 Corinthians 10:13, also wrote 2 Corinthians 1:8, where he reports, "about the trouble we went through in the province of Asia. We were crushed and overwhelmed beyond our ability to endure, and we thought we would never live through it. In fact, we expected to die. But as a result, we stopped relying on ourselves and learned to rely only on God, who raises the dead." It is clear from this verse, that apostle Paul understood that we can indeed face trials and temptations that are beyond our ability to endure in our own strength.

So, what did he mean in 1 Corinthians 10:13? One of my friends provide helpful insight. He pointed out that regardless of how fierce the devil's temptations are, they are limited to what is common to man, meaning that they do not have supernatural power attached to them. But, our spiritual defenses and weapons are not limited to what is common to man. We have access to God's unlimited, supernatural power, and our weapons and spiritual defenses have unlimited, supernatural power attached to them. In 2 Corinthians 10:4 the Bible states that our weapons are mighty through God. So, there is nothing the devil can throw at us that we are not equipped to handle in God's strength, because we are combating natural power with supernatural power. Our steadfast trust in God's faithfulness empowers us to overcome every temptation of the devil.

Every Sin is an Identity Crisis Issue

Every sin is a choice to act contrary to our identity as children of God. It is a choice to deny who we are in Christ and choose to act inconsistent with the nature of God in us. Every sin is acting contrary to our divine DNA. Apostle James gives a detailed description of the trajectory and progression of sin. He says, "Every one is tempted when he is drawn away by his own desires and enticed. Then, when desire has conceived, it gives birth to sin; and sin, when it is full-grown, brings forth death." (James 1: 14-15).

> *Every sin is a choice to act contrary to our identity as children of God.*

Every temptation appeals to an active or latent desire, lust or craving in you. The devil sinks the lure into your mind and attempts to reel you in. Then the battle ensues, the battle between the flesh and the spirit. Before we were saved, our bodies were conditioned to living according to the dictates of this world, and our souls were conformed to the pattern of this world, until we gave our lives to Christ. Thereafter, whenever our body wants to do things the way of the world, the Holy Spirit would intervene and impart the word and will of God about that situation to our soul.

Galatians 5:17, describes this behind the scenes conflict between the flesh and the Spirit. It states that the sinful flesh in us wants to do evil, which is just the opposite of what the Spirit wants. And the Spirit gives us desires that are the opposite of what the flesh desires. These two forces are constantly fighting each other.

During temptation, this conflict escalates. On the one hand we have the strong urging of the Holy Spirit to make a choice that honors God, but on the other hand, we are bullied by the flesh's craving, lust and desire to choose sin. We can go with the flesh, and the information it receives from the five senses; and choose sin; or we can affirm our new nature in Christ by obeying the prompting of Holy Spirit to choose what is right.

This conflict precipitates a crisis, an identity crisis. The choice we make reveals our understanding of our identity and who is boss in our lives. The Bible tells us to put off our former way of life, our old self, that is corrupt according to its sinful desires and to put on our new way of life, the new person recreated in Christ in true righteousness and holiness. This is an ongoing process of sanctification that begins at the new birth and continues throughout life. When we give our lives to Christ, the power of sin is immediately broken. We have the power through the Holy Spirit to overcome sin and say no to its dictates. But our minds have been conditioned to think in a certain way and needs to be reprogrammed with information from the Spirit of God and our new nature.

As we grow in Christ, we increase in our knowledge of the word of God, our ability to hear and obey the voice of God, and our understanding of our new identity in Christ. So, there should be a progressive manifestation of victory over sin in our lives. When we persist in choosing sin, we belie the life of God in us. Every time we say yes to sin, we are denying our identity in Christ. Our habitual, willful, sinful choices call into question whether we were ever saved. It shows that we truly do not know who we are and whose we are.

First John 3:9 says it best, "No one born of God deliberately, knowingly, and habitually practices sin, for God's nature abides in him, His principle of life, the divine sperm, remains permanently within him; and he cannot practice sinning because he is born of God." 1 John 3:9 AMPC.

Every time we choose sin, we have to step over our identity in Christ to commit it!

CHAPTER 7
THE INNER MAN

On a hot summer afternoon in June of 2018, I was in the closet of a local school surrounded by boxes and boxes of puzzles. A couple years before that, my church had started a community outreach where we would "adopt" a local school and during the summer, when the kids were on vacation, our church would organize a school makeover. The massive project included cleaning and repainting classrooms, rebuilding dilapidated structures, re-carpeting offices, power washing, gardening, mulching, planting flowers, purchasing needed equipment, and much more. Over time, this became a big community event that blessed area schools and glorified the name of the Lord. In 2018, our adopted school was a local school for the deaf, and my first assignment for the day was to organize the teachers closet.

I had never seen so many puzzles in one place! There were puzzles of all shapes, colors and sizes, from a few large pieces, to hundreds of tiny pieces. My job was to find the right puzzle pieces, put them in the right box and organize the boxes neatly on the shelves. It was quite a sight! I and my daughter were on the floor, on our hands and knees, surrounded by puzzle pieces and trying very diligently to find where they fit. As we worked, I wondered about the kids who played with these puzzles and their glee when they found the pieces that fit. I pondered the frustration of having a piece that you think is perfectly shaped like the slot in front of you, and you try to force it into that slot, but it just wouldn't fit! I mused at how, when finally, all the pieces are in place, and you insert that last piece that completes the puzzle; now you can declare victory, sit back, and gaze at the beautiful picture that is revealed!

Do you know that you are like a puzzle piece? Do you know that you are specially and uniquely designed by God for placement in a certain type of job or ministry where you can thrive? Do you know that God has given you a distinctive, inborn identity that determines how you interact with your environment, as well as your strengths, weaknesses, interests, and even hobbies? The answer to all those questions is YES, and the key is in the "inner man".

The Inner Man

Man is a spiritual being created by God with a precise order and balance of spirit, soul, and body. Ephesians 2:10 states that we are God's handiwork, a re-created people that will fulfil the destiny that He has for each of us. Even before we were born, God planned in advance our destiny and the good works we would do to fulfill it. Then He put in us, the unique combination of "self" that will enable us to achieve this purpose. The Greek word translated as handiwork or workmanship is the word "poema" from which we derive the English word poem. So, this verse is saying that we are God's masterpiece, His artistic creation. God is the master designer, the supreme artist, and we are His work of art, His poem. A poem is a thing of beauty, eloquence, and grace. God reproduced Himself in us, and wants us to be an eloquent expression of His beauty and grace. David captured this vividly when he said, "You created my inmost being; you knit me together in my mother's womb. I praise you because I am fearfully and wonderfully made; your works are wonderful, I know that full well. (Psalms 139:13-14).

> *The inner man is made up of the personality, character, and temperament.*

Components of the Inner Man

In 2 Corinthians 4:16, apostle Paul states, "Therefore, we do not lose heart, but though our outer man is decaying, yet our inner man is being renewed day by day. Here, he makes a distinction between the "outer man", the body; and the "inner man". According to the National Christian Counselors Association, the inner man is made up of the personality, character, and temperament. Character is learned behavior, and can be changed during one's lifetime through an act of the will, self-awareness, self-discipline and the work of the Holy Spirit. Character reflects our temperament and its interaction with our environment. Personality is how we present ourselves to the world. This portrayal can be an unconscious image selection or one chosen as an act of the will.

Often, "personality" is a mask that we wear and can vary with different settings. Though it has a measure of reality, it is not completely honest. Personality incorporates the strategies we learned and adopted to survive in the world, including our self-protection mechanisms, and behaviors we employ to get us what we want or need. This is why people may act one way at the office or in public and another way at home. Temperament on the other hand is the inborn part of us, which remains the same, regardless of what public persona we adopt. We can respond for a while out of our personality, but ultimately our temperament and character reveal who we really are. (LaCour).

> There are five basic temperaments, the Choleric, Sanguine, Phlegmatic, Melancholy, and Supine; and over four thousand temperament blends.

Five Basic Temperaments

There are five basic temperaments, the Choleric, Sanguine, Phlegmatic, Melancholy and Supine; and over four thousand temperament blends.

Choleric is the hot, quick, active, practical and strong willed temperament. Cholerics are driven, self-sufficient, and fiercely independent. They are self-starters, goal oriented, practical, and capable of making sound decisions. Cholerics are natural born leaders. They are quick to recognize and take advantage of opportunities, have a dogged determination, and often succeed where others fail. However, Cholerics lack empathy, mercy, and compassion, and love is often not high on their list of priorities. Because Cholerics can achieve so much, they often have no sympathy for those who can't.

Sanguine is the warm, buoyant, lively, and fun-loving temperament. Sanguines are extroverts and the life of the party. For them, feelings rather than reflective thoughts predominate in decision formation. The sanguine is never at a loss for words, though he or she often speaks without thinking things through. Sanguines are not very organized, and can readily forget appointments, responsibilities and obligations. They can be noisy, blustery, friendly, energetic, and lovable.

Phlegmatic is the calm, cool, easygoing, and well balanced temperament. Phlegmatics have a very high boiling point and never seem to be ruffled or angry. They are very consistent and keep their emotions under control. They enjoy people, have a dry sense of humor, and are quite adept at avoiding as much involvement as possible. They are reluctant leaders, but when roused into action, they are very competent and passionate. Phlegmatics are not risktakers. They are well organized, work well under pressure, and are very dependable.

Melancholy is the analytical, self-sacrificing, gifted, perfectionist, with a very sensitive, emotional nature. Melancholics are introverts and can be moody. They do not make friends easily, but when made, are very loyal and faithful. They are very dependable, thorough and precise, and their exceptional analytical abilities enable them to accurately diagnose the pitfalls of any project. Melancholics tend to have high intellectual energies, creativity and imagination.

Supine is the quiet, very accommodating, "loves to serve" temperament. Supines are both introverted and extroverted, have a servant's heart, appear to be withdrawn and are often in the background. They like people, have a great capacity for service, and possess an inborn gentle spirit. They are dependable, excellent followers, "rule enforcers", and absolutely loyal. They are not very strong willed, are not great at decision making, and struggle with low self-esteem.

> *Temperament is the inborn part of man that determines how we react to people, places, and things.*

Why is Temperament Important to Identity?

Temperament is a core component of your "inner man". It is your God-created, God-given, unique identity, and the basic building block of character. It is your internal wiring by God that prepares you to fulfill His purpose for your life. According to the National Christian Counselors Association, our God created temperament is the inborn part of man that determines how we react to people, places, and things. It is how we interact with the world around us. Our temperament affects our perception of ourselves, the people who love us, and our relationship with God Himself. Our ability to accomplish tasks, make decisions, relate to people and handle stress are tied to our temperament. Also, individual temperament determines our basic emotional needs, and how we respond when those needs are not met. Simply stated, our temperament traits set the "tone and rhythm" by which we live our lives. (LaCour).

Human beings have physical needs, like the need for food, water, and shelter, to maintain the physical body, and if these needs go unmet, the physical body will break down and die. In the same way, God has put in each person a temperament or temperament blends that have needs. If these needs are not met, the individual will break down emotionally. So, identifying each individual's temperament, the associated temperament needs, and how to meet those needs in godly ways, will equip and empower them to grow personally, relationally, and spiritually.

> *Temperament is "spiritual genetics" or God's imprint in you.*

Temperament is "spiritual genetics" or God's imprint in you. So, knowledge of your inborn temperament or temperament blends is an important part of your identity. It helps you to understand yourself, and know why you do what you do. It pinpoints your self-perception and perception of others, and is the determining factor in how well you interact with people, and handle the stresses and pressures of life. Temperament and the needs within each temperament not only determines and controls the level and freedom of your interaction with people; it also controls the level of your interaction with God the Father, the Lord Jesus Christ and the Holy Spirit. It dictates how free you feel to respond to God's love, how openly you worship Him or how freely you accept the grace, joy, and peace He offers; or reject them because of feelings of unworthiness. Temperament can help detect areas where you are vulnerable to spiritual setbacks and emotional breakdown.

Temperament is a determining factor in:
1. How you interact with your family and friends
2. How you interact in a dating relationship and the pitfalls
3. Finding a career that is most suitable for you
4. Identifying hobbies that will interest and fulfill you
5. How you make decisions and take on responsibility
6. How dependent or independent you are, and
7. Your spiritual development and growth

In sum, your temperament is a critical piece of your identity and understanding your temperament is key to understanding yourself and your behavior. It unlocks the door to your purpose, and provides insight into the proclivities and propensities that could derail and destroy you. Temperament Therapy helps to identify your internal wiring in the areas of Inclusion - social orientation and intellectual energies; Control - decision making and responsibility; and Affection - love, approval, and deep relationships. (*Arno*).

> *Temperament Therapy helps to identify your internal wiring in the areas of Inclusion, Control, and Affection.*

Temperament is Transformational to Identity

Last year, a beautiful, sweet, woman approached me with a request. Let's call her Jane. She and I had connected through my weekly GraceTalk show. She sent me an email in which she said:

> "I would like you to pray about discipling me to whatever extent God allows. Honestly, I do not have a clue what this would entail or look like, but during tonight's show, the talk of discipleship rang through me like a confirmation of need more than a call to serve, although I recognize this call as well. I feel like I am floundering spiritually as I navigate many new things in my life. It is more a lack of direction that seems to thwart any progress in advancing and taking ground for the kingdom of God, rather than a desire to do so. I do not see myself as a powerful part of the family. I see shame, fear, doubt, and lack of purpose, but I cannot seem to pray or study to an end that draws me closer to Jesus and closer to understanding the calling He has for my days. This has not stopped me from reaching out, sharing, joining groups,

and studying, but I know there is something more God desires to reveal to, in, and through me. My hope is that a connection in a disciple-like relationship would shed light on the direction God has for me to walk in. I can see that you fill many roles and that your Source is Christ Himself when you minister. Please prayerfully consider a way that would allow for a period of mentoring."

I sought the Lord about her request, and with His go-ahead, Jane and I entered into a mentoring relationship. At our first meeting, I was amazed by how many lies she had come to believe about herself. Here before me was this beautiful, kind, accomplished and articulate woman. She is a high school teacher and spends her days helping kids to achieve their God-given potential. I personally believe teachers are like angels among us! The patience, love and grace that they dole out lavishly, on a daily basis, is nothing short of divine! Plus, my mom was a grade school teacher. Some of my fondest memories are of being out and about with her and running into one of her former students. Again, and again, they would call out to her in a voice of happy surprise, hurry over, and remind her of who they were. So many times, I watched as the look of puzzlement on my mom's face transformed into a look of astonishment and sheer joy as she looked at her former student, now a grown adult! My mom would beam with pride as they told her how they have gone on to succeed in life. She would sometimes tear up when she learned, first-hand, from these former students, what an impact she had made on them in grade school. Those encounters were always richly rewarding, and left an indelible impression on me.

So, I was taken aback as I looked at this precious woman, who worked as a grade school teacher, and heard her tell me that she was not benefiting anyone, that she is a disappointment, is not good enough, will never lose weight, will never quit smoking, and that she was too broken, unwanted, unfixable, useless, and disposable. She went on to say that God was disappointed with her, and that her prayers were not worth hearing. She felt disconnected and distant from God, and unable to feel or receive His love.

Many of these lies are so blatantly false, and the premise so factually, objectively and verifiably wrong, but yet she believed them so completely. She had plenty of pervasive fears as well that clouded her thought process. Over time, this wrong thinking became a stronghold that erected a major barrier between her, other people, and God. She also shared that she had a tough time making decisions, and was dependent on other people to lead and provide direction and structure for her life. Needless to say, she had a lot of self-loathing, low self-esteem, and inferiority; and as a result, she hid herself.

Unbeknownst to her, I am studying for a Ph.D. in Christian counseling, and at that time, I was also training to become a Certified Temperament Counselor. (I have since become certified as a Professional Christian Counselor, Certified Temperament Counselor, and a Licensed Clinical Pastoral Counselor). Part of my training was an in-depth study of Temperament Theory and Temperament Therapy. In the course of our mentoring sessions, I shared with her about inborn temperaments and that our discussions have led me to believe that she has the Supine temperament. I explained that the indecision, low self-esteem, inferiority and negative perception of herself were the weaknesses of that temperament. However, the temperament also has many strengths and if she submitted to God, she could use the tools that God provided in His word to overcome her temperament weaknesses and become the person God created her to be.

The Supine temperament is relatively new. It was identified and researched by the National Christian Counselors Association in 1984. Many people know about temperaments generally, as one of the building blocks of identity, and knowledge about the four basic temperaments – Choleric, Sanguine, Melancholy and Phlegmatic – go as far back as Hippocrates. However, the Supine temperament is little known. I learned of it through my studies. Jane had never heard of it. But she immediately went to work and researched it on the internet. I also later administered the Arno Profile System (APS) temperament assessment to her, and sure enough, she was mostly a Supine, with some temperament blends.

The knowledge of her unique temperament design by God set her free. The impact was dramatic! She writes:

"Regarding learning of the Supine temperament and how it is my very own, chosen by God temperament: It reminded me of a Facebook post about a woman with a birth deformity who, as an adult, found a support group and realized she was not alone. She began to let herself be seen for who she was made to be. I pondered and saw that we are ALL flawed for this world, but not at all in the heavenlies. The key is to simply live in the heavenly realm where we are perfectly and wonderfully made. I have a temperament and a personality that has weaknesses in the here and now, but is part of who I am in the eternity that is already begun. I have hidden myself because I saw my personality as broken and wrong and flawed, but I feel like I have been taken out and put on a shelf to be seen, not for what I appear to be, but because I am loved by the Maker. And He will display his wonderful creation just as she is made to be. I may need to ask for dusting and polishing from the dirt from this world, but the creation itself is perfect and a delight to God. I still need to learn how to be comfortable in that light and not hide myself from myself, from others, and from God. But, now I know that I will learn this and so much more."

Her Prayer: Lord, "Show me how to connect with the authentic me, the way You made me to be. Let me stand on my own two feet to move forward to fulfill Your plan, purpose, and agenda. This is Your work, no one can do it but you. Do it! Have your way. Help me to lean in and seek Your face, trust You, decode what I heard tonight, unpack it, and apply it. Do what only You can do. Only Your word can work. Put Your word to work in me" Amen!

Since that time, Jane is undergoing transformation and connecting with her true identity in Christ! The key that unlocked her transformation was learning about her "inner man". She has grown in personal confidence, poise and self-esteem. She is more self-aware, self-accepting, and happier. The mental and emotional shackles that held her bound are beginning to fall off, and she is allowing herself to be the woman that God created her to be. She still has negative thoughts about herself and still feels the hesitation and self-doubt; but she is learning to recognize these as temperament weaknesses and how to apply the word of God to overcome them. Most importantly, she does not let those voices stop her. Knowledge of her temperament unlocked the potential that was in her and powered her personal growth and breakthrough. This transformation process is still ongoing, not only for her, but for all of us. We are in the process of becoming, becoming who we are; the men and women God created us to be. For Jane, she is well on her way, and she is not alone. In my counseling ministry, I have seen Temperament Therapy transform lives, rebuild families, and heal dysfunctional relationships.

Temperament and the Kingdom of God

The kingdom of God is like a giant jigsaw puzzle. Each person is tailor-made for a certain position, and only when they are properly placed in their slots will they be happy and fulfilled, and God's beautiful picture for their lives be revealed. Learning about temperament will help each individual understand their inner man, and find the unique identity, talents, abilities, and place designed for them by God.

Each temperament has a unique role and fit in the kingdom of God. First Corinthians 12 states that the body of Christ is just like the human body. It has many parts which make up one body, and God has put each part just where He wants it. The following is an illustration of the role different temperaments can play in the kingdom.

> *Each temperament has a unique role and fit in the kingdom of God.*

The doorway into the kingdom of God is saving faith in Jesus Christ as Lord and Savior. Jesus said, "you must be born again." There's no temperament better suited for the gatekeeper role than the Sanguine. Jesus commanded all Christians to be witnesses, but Sanguines make the best evangelists! Their delightful, charismatic personality, and passionate presentation of the gospel has inspired multitudes and led millions to Christ. A great example is apostle Peter who preached and thousands came to Christ.

While the Sanguine moves on to the next crusade or evangelistic outreach, in his wake, there are multitudes of new Christians who need to be fed, trained, and discipled. This is where the Melancholics step in. Their patience, self-sacrifice, intellect, and sensitive nature are used by the Holy Spirit to teach, disciple, encourage, and help young converts to grow in their walk with Christ. Melancholics also make excellent worship leaders, prayer ministers, and much more. A great example is apostle John who discipled converts whom he called "My dear children".

The success of the Sanguine and the Melancholy lead to growth in the church. Souls are being added to the kingdom and they are learning and growing! Now we need new churches, programs, ministries, events, facilities, and buildings to support the work. Who better to do this than the hard driving Choleric! Their boundless energy, enthusiasm, leadership, and unstoppable drive are exactly what is needed for planning and executing these projects, raising funds, and mobilizing people to work. A great example is apostle Paul who planted churches throughout the known world of his time.

The work of the Sanguine, Melancholy, and Choleric has led to tremendous growth and breakthrough. God is moving, people are being set free, and the kingdom of God is expanding. This expansion brings tons of "behind the scenes" work. We need program coordinators, computer systems analysts, researchers, video editors, data analytics, administrative support, accountants, and audio-visual professionals. Nobody is better suited for this work of precision, accuracy, and detail like the Phlegmatic. A great example is Stephen who organized the food program in the early church.

With growth, increased church ministry and impact, come life challenges and the need for men and women with a servant's heart to care for the hurting, minister to the sick, help the needy, visit the nursing homes and shut ins, serve the homeless, and outreach to prisons and hospitals. No one can fill this role better than the Supine! The men and women whose hearts God has filled with a great capacity to serve the church and community in the name of the Lord. A great example is Martha. Everywhere you see her in the Bible, she is serving.

As stated earlier, there are five basic temperaments and over 4000 temperament blends. So, the above is a very simplified illustration of the role that different temperaments can play in the body of Christ. The individual temperaments and temperament blends in the areas of Inclusion, Control, and Affection, account for the placement of the individual in the role that God had ordained for them.

As a Temperament Counselor, and Licensed Clinical Pastoral Counselor, I help people to know themselves, understand their unique inner workings, resolve internal stress, address external and relational issues, and locate the unique placement God has designed for them as far as their job, career, and service in the body of Christ.

> *For a person to reach spiritual maturity, the emotional part of them must interact with God to meet their emotional needs, and they must lean on God's strength to overcome their temperament weaknesses.*

God created us with emotional needs that only He can meet. He also gave us temperaments with weaknesses that only He can strengthen. For a person to reach spiritual maturity, the emotional part of them must interact with God to meet their emotional needs, and they must lean on God's strength to overcome their temperament weaknesses. This is what apostle Paul meant when he said, "I take pleasure in my weaknesses, for when I am weak, then I am strong" (2 Corinthians 12:10). This is the power of Christ working in and through us.

One of the blessings of understanding temperament is the realization that no human being can meet all of our temperament needs, all of the time. As we grow in God, we can learn to reduce our reliance on people and transfer our dependence to God. He alone can meet our deepest needs.

CHAPTER 8
THE GOD KIND

Often, we hear teachings or read articles about the "God kind" of faith, life, love or other godly attribute. A "kind" describes a group of people or things that have similar nature, characteristics, attributes or elements; things that are of the same sort, class, species or order. So, what does it mean that we are the God kind? It means that we are like God, having His attributes and nature, and capable of manifesting His power.

"In Genesis 1, we see a pattern. When God wanted to create anything, he spoke to the source of the thing. In verse 11 God said: "Let the land sprout with vegetation. . . And it was so." In verse 20 God said, "Let the waters swarm with fish and other life . . . and . . . Let the skies be filled with birds of every kind. . . And it was so." In verse 24, God said, "Let the earth bring forth every sort of animal. . . And it was so." The pattern is, God speaks to the source of the thing to be created to bring forth and it brought forth. When it came time to make man, God spoke to Himself. He said, "Let us make man in our image, according to our likeness." God is our source of origin, not tadpoles, a big bang, or anything else. Mankind came from God. We are His offspring (Acts 17:28).

First John 4:17(b) states, that as He, Jesus is, so are we in this world. We are made in the image and likeness of God. An image is an authentic representation of a person or thing and likeness is the capacity to resemble, replicate, or reproduce that person or thing. We are an authentic representation of God in the earth and have the capacity to reproduce Him, His love, character, grace, and other attributes on the earth. God is our source and He reproduced us after His kind. We are the God-kind.

The Genetic Code

DNA contains the genetic code, organizing principle and information for all living organisms. It is self-replicating material, the main constituent of chromosomes, and the carrier of genetic information. It is passed from parents to offspring, and determines the physical and mental capabilities, traits, attributes, pre-disposition and other characteristics of an individual. Several Bible passages tell us that we are God's sons and daughters. We are a chip off the old block. We are royalty!

> *God is our source and He reproduced us after His kind. We are the God-kind.*

Second Peter 2:9 declares that we are a chosen generation, a royal priesthood, a holy nation, God's own special people. A divine refrain that is repeated over and over again in the old testament is, "I will be a Father to you, and you shall be my sons and daughters". In the New Testament, 2 Corinthians 6:18 states it emphatically, "I will be a Father to you, and you shall be My sons and daughters, says the LORD Almighty." It is abundantly clear that Fatherhood is the heart of God and He has placed tremendous value in us as His sons and daughters. If God is our Father, then His divine DNA would be in us. Let's take a look into the divine DNA and identify the genetic material that is handed down to us from our heavenly Father.

The Person of God: Let's start with the basics. God is a living person, with breath, a mind, a will and emotions. He is not a "force" or "power" or "essence". He is not diffused into and one with the "universe". He is a real, separate, and distinct being; with attributes, personality and intelligence. He is the creator of the universe. He has a personal name, in fact, He has many names. He can be personally known and intimately loved; and does Himself personally know and intimately love. God is a person!

God is a Spirit: Jesus, speaking in John 4:24, confirms this truth. He said that God is a Spirit, and those who worship or commune with Him must do so in spirit and in truth. Being a Spirit means that Father God does not have flesh and blood. He does not have the limitations imposed by the physical body, but it also means that He is not subject to the physical sensory perceptions of the human body. So, we cannot contact God with our five natural senses. We cannot routinely see, hear, touch, taste or smell God with our physical senses. First Timothy 6:16 states that no man has seen or can see God. This is why Hebrews 11:6 declares that without faith it is impossible to please God. For anyone who comes to God must believe that He exists, and is a rewarder of those who diligently seek him. We must believe that God exists, because we can't see him with our physical eyes.

Even though we cannot routinely contact God with our physical senses, the Bible clearly states that we can perceive God. David said that we can "taste and see" that God is good (Psalm 34:8). Isaiah said, "I saw the Lord, sitting upon a throne, high and lifted up"

(Isaiah 6:1). Several Bible characters heard God speak to them: Abraham in Genesis 12;1, Moses in Exodus 33:11; Samuel in 1 Samuel 3:7-11; and apostle Paul in Acts 9:4. Today, the Holy Spirit lives inside believers and is in constant contact with us in our spirits. So, we can "see" God with the eyes of our heart; He can reveal Himself in a vision or dream; and we can hear His voice in our spirits and through His word. Jesus said, my sheep hear my voice (John 10:27). In Isaiah 41:13, God promises to take us by the hand and lead us; and in Philippians 3:10, the Bible says that we can know God through a personal relationship. It's like the hymn writer said, "And He walks with me, and He talks with me, and He tells me that I am His own." We can have a personal, intimate relationship with Almighty God.

This fact, that God is a Spirit, is a very important point. It sets the context for our relationship with God. He is a spirit and so, to know, connect with, relate to, and fellowship with him, we must engage Him in the spirit. We must be able to see in the spirit, speak spirit, and hear with spiritual ears. This is why the Bible says on several occasions, "let him that has ears to hear, hear what the Spirit is saying". It is not talking about physical ears, but ability to hear and perceive in the spirit. First Corinthians 2:14 makes this point very clearly: "But the natural man does not receive the things of the Spirit of God, for they are foolishness to him; nor can he know them, because they are spiritually discerned." Put simply, only those who are spiritual can understand what the Spirit says.

Natural beings give birth to natural beings. God is a spirit, so He gives birth to spiritual beings. When we are born into God's family, it is a spiritual birth. This explains the exchange between Nicodemus and Jesus in John 3. He thought Jesus was talking about natural rebirth and asked incredulously, "how can a man enter his mother's womb and be born again?" Jesus explained, "Humans can reproduce only human life, but the Holy Spirit gives birth to spiritual life". Because God is a Spirit, He gave birth to us in the spirit. The Bible states that when a person is in Christ, he or she is a new creation. Obviously, this is not a physical reality, because your physical body did not change when you became born again. However, it is a profound and radical spiritual reality; you became a brand new creation in the spirit. God's Spirit came into your heart to reside, and to enable you to connect with and relate to Him.

> *The extent to which we are willing to engage with and in the spirit realm, will determine our capacity to know, see, contact, build a relationship with, and experience God.*

This leads us to this most important point, that the extent to which we are willing to engage with and in the spirit realm, will determine our capacity to know, see, contact, build a relationship with and experience God. So many Christians are trying so hard to "feel", see, audibly hear, and connect with God in the natural sense that they miss out on the key revelation that all of God's provisions and abundance are available to us in the spirit realm (Ephesians 1:3). God can and does occasionally make His presence manifest, such that we can hear Him audibly or "see" him visibly, or "feel" his presence; but those occurrences are not intended to be an everyday staple experience. God is a spirit, speaks spirit, lives in the spirit world and wants to be known as a spirit. To know Him we must activate our spirit, learn to speak spirit, know who we are in the spirit, and relate with him by and through our spirits. We can walk with Him, talk with Him, and fellowship with Him, in His world, the spirit world.

"To "speak spirit" means, firstly, speaking the word of God. In John 6:63, Jesus said, "And the very words I have spoken to you are spirit and life". When we speak the word of God, we are speaking words "which the Holy Spirit teaches" and bringing the life of God into the situation. The word of God is spirit, so, when we proclaim the word of God, we cut through every obstruction, barrier or hindrance in the spirit realm and gain direct access to the resources God has provided for us. Secondly, to "speak spirit" means, speaking in tongues. Acts 2:4 explains: "And everyone present was filled with the Holy Spirit and began speaking in other languages, or in other tongues, as the Holy Spirit gave them this ability." So, speaking in tongues is speaking the language of the Holy Spirit. Again, it cuts through every impediment or barrier and nothing is lost in the translation. When we speak or pray in tongues, we are talking, spirit to spirit." (*Godson*).

> *When we speak or pray in tongues, we are talking to God, spirit to spirit.*

I cannot conclude this chapter without pointing out that while God the Father and Holy Spirit are spirits, God the son, Jesus, does have a body. In John chapter 4, when He taught us that God is a spirit, He Himself was in a physical body at that time. When He rose from the dead, He resurrected with a glorified body, and today, in heaven, He is still in a glorified, physical body. This means that He has a body that can be touched and felt. After His resurrection, while speaking to His fear stricken disciples who thought He was a ghost, Jesus said, "Why are you so frightened? Don't let doubt enter your hearts. See my pierced hands and feet. See for yourselves, it is I, standing here alive. Touch me and know that my wounds are real. A spirit does not have a body of flesh and bone as you see that I have." Then he showed them his pierced hands and feet and let them touch his wounds" (Luke 24:39).

The glorious truth is that we have a man in heaven, Jesus Christ the "Son of man" and the Son of God!

CHAPTER 9
THE DIVINE DNA

God is Eternal: God has existed from the beginning. He is the beginning. There was never a time when God was not, and there will never be a time when God is not. He always was and always will be. He is the Alpha and Omega, the beginning and the end. He is eternal! The Bible makes no attempt to explain God. It simply declares Him. Genesis 1:1 begins with the powerful proclamation; "In the beginning, God…" He is self-existing. He was not created and can never cease to exist. He simply is, in and of Himself, by Himself, independently, without cause, or origin or end. This is called aseity, the self-existence of Almighty God.

God is a Tripartite Being: He is three persons in one, three distinct and co-equal persons. God the Father, God the Son, and God the Holy Spirit, make up the Godhead, the trinity. Even though the scriptures attest to the fact of a triune God (Matthew 3:16-17; 2 Corinthians 13:14), this truth can be hard to grasp. A simplified way to understand this is to look in the mirror. God made us like Himself, and so, we are tripartite beings. We are a spirit, we have a soul and we live in a physical body (1 Thessalonians 5:23).

One of the things I love to do at church is to teach young people the word of God. I gave my life to Christ as a youth, so I have a passion for reaching kids with the gospel. Also, I believe that while the salvation of every soul is critical, of eternal consequence and inestimable value, saving the souls of kids has the potential for tremendous profit, because unlike an adult, kids can devote their entire lifetime to serving God and building His kingdom. But another reason I like to teach kids, is that they can grasp spiritual truth with simple faith. When I taught them about the trinity, it was a very smelly class! I brought in hard boiled eggs, and explained how the yolk, the egg white and the shell are distinct parts, but altogether make one whole egg. They got it, and ate it too!

God is Transcendent and Immanent: He is set apart from human beings. He is a cut above. He is God all by Himself. He is in a category of one. There is nobody else like Him. God is immanent in the world He created. This means that He is inherent, pervasive and innately indwelling the universe. All of creation acknowledges and declares His presence, power, and glory. Psalm 19:1-4; states that "The heavens proclaim the glory of God. The skies display his craftsmanship. Day after day they continue to speak; night after night they make him known. They speak without a sound or word; their voice is never heard. Yet their message has gone throughout the earth, and their words to all the world." In Romans 1:19-20, apostle Paul emphasized this point. Speaking of humanity, he states that, "They know the truth about God because he has made it obvious to them. For ever since the world was created, people have seen the earth and sky. Through everything God made, they can clearly see his invisible qualities—his eternal power and divine nature. So they have no excuse for not knowing God." God is immanent. All of creation knows and proclaims Him. you should too!

God is Omni: Omnipotent, Omnipresent, and Omniscient:

God is Omnipotent. He is all powerful and nothing is impossible for Him. He is infinite and limitless in ability, capacity, strength, might, potential, and prowess. He said of Himself, "I am the God of all flesh, is anything too hard for me?" God has all power and authority. He can do anything! God is omnipresent. God's presence is continuous and ubiquitous throughout all of creation. He is present everywhere at the same time, though it may not be revealed in the same way, at the same time, to people everywhere. God is omniscient. He has all knowledge. He knows everything there is to know about everything and everyone, and He knows it all at the same time. God cannot become wiser, stronger or more knowledgeable. Isaiah 40:28-29, outlines the omniscience of God. It asks rhetorically, "Have you never heard? Have you never understood? The LORD is the everlasting God, the Creator of all the earth. He never grows weak or weary. No one can measure the depths of his understanding. He gives power to the weak and strength to the powerless." In Psalm 139:7-12, David marvels at the omnipresence of God. He muses, "I can never escape from your Spirit! I can never get away from your presence! If I go up to heaven, you are there; if I go down to the grave, you are there. If I ride the wings of the morning, if I dwell by the farthest oceans, even there your hand will guide me, and your strength will support me. I could ask the darkness to hide me and the light around me to become night—but even in darkness I cannot hide from you. To you the night shines as bright as day. Darkness and light are the same to you".

> *One name of God that deftly captures His omni attributes, is the name "I AM".*

One name of God that deftly captures His omni attributes, is the name "I AM". God is and can be any and everything we need Him to be; at any time, and all at the same time. He can be any and everywhere, He knows any and everything, and He can do any and everything. He is inexhaustible! He knows no limitations except the ones that He has voluntarily placed on Himself. For example, God cannot lie. His divine nature, moral uprightness, righteousness and infinite holiness bar Him from ever speaking or acting a lie. Also, God has limited Himself to what He said in His word. He will not go outside His word. He will only do what He has said in His word.

The other names of God, like Abba, El-Shaddai, Jehovah Shammah, Nissi, Rophe, Tsidkenu, Jireh, Adonai, Roi, Elohim, Yahweh, and more, all reveal aspects of his omnipotence, omnipresence and omniscience. In the New Testament, one name that captures the omni attributes of God is YESHUA, JESUS, the name above all names! He is the great I AM! And at His name, every knee shall bow, in heaven and on earth and under the earth, and every tongue declare that He is Lord.

God is NOT a Man

If we don't see God correctly, we will not have a right relationship with Him.

The sum total of the person of God is this, God is not a man. God is God. This might appear to be an obvious statement, but it is pregnant with meaning. We tend to forget that God is not man, and comparing God to man is one of the key strategies of the devil to tempt and discourage us. So many times, the devil has worked in the lives of Christians to make us resentful toward God. He accuses

God in our hearts. He whispers, "If God really loved you, why did He not deliver you from that terrible situation? If He really cares, why did He let you go through that? Think about it, if it was your child and you had all power to stop that from happening to them, wouldn't you? If you could keep them from all that hurt, wouldn't you? God doesn't love you, He doesn't care, and He cannot be trusted to take care of you." And we listen; we listen to the devil's taunts because it makes sense to our natural minds. And we agree with the devil and conclude that God doesn't care. A related strategy of the devil is to make us view the love of our perfect heavenly Father through the lens of the flawed love, failings, imperfections, and failures of our earthly fathers. This distorts our view of God, and if we don't see God correctly, we will not have a right relationship with Him.

> *One singular proof that God is not man is that He sent His only son to die for sinful, rebellious mankind.*

The disconnect is that we are expecting God to act like a man and we are judging him by human standards. The problem with that line of thought is that the Bible states clearly that God is not a man (Numbers 23:19). It couldn't be more plain. Accusing God of not acting like a human being to deliver you the way you would act to deliver your natural child, is completely missing the point that God acts with a perspective far beyond what any human being can see, perceive or understand. God's vantage point is all of humanity, all of time and all of eternity. Isaiah 55 emphasizes the point, that God's ways and thoughts are much higher than ours. He takes into account not just the micro issue you are dealing with, but the macro issues, eternal impacts, ripple effects, all the interconnections with and interconnectedness of all of humanity, and the implications, not only for now, but for all time and eternity. We should be thankful that God is not man! One singular proof that God is not man is that He sent His only son to die for sinful, rebellious mankind. I do not know of any human being who would willingly subject their child, talk less of their only child, to horrendous torture and death like the one Jesus endured, to save mankind. God is not a man, and thank God that He isn't! If God were a man, we would still be in our sins, and condemned to eternal damnation.

> *God's vantage point is all of humanity, all of time and all of eternity.*

Don't let the enemy deceive you. God loves and cares for you. He sees you, knows you by name, and is intimately acquainted with your pain. His plan is the best for you, given all He sees and knows. He is working on your behalf and will redeem your situation for your blessing, and His glory. He will use what the devil meant for evil, and turn it around for your good. What do you need God to be for you today? What battle do you need Him to fight in your life? Call upon the GREAT I AM, and He will show up and show off on your behalf. The Bible is clear! God is not a man, so He does not lie. He is not human, so He does not change His mind. He has never spoken and failed to act. He has never promised and failed to carry it through. So, we can completely trust Him and rest in the unfailing love and character of our heavenly Father.

The Nature of God: His Innate Attributes

Creator: Our first introduction to God is as creator. It is the nature of God to create. Romans 4:17 states that He creates new things out of nothing, gives life to the dead, and calls those things which do not exist as though they did. We first meet Him in Genesis creating the world with His spoken word. "Genesis chapter 1 is repeatedly punctuated by two sets of three words, "And God said" and, "And God called". And everything that God said or called came into physical manifestation, every single time! By the end of that chapter, the entire universe had been created, by the power of the spoken word" of God. (*Fight to Win*). God is the creator of all things in three realms; in heaven, on earth and beneath the earth.

God is Holy: To be holy is to be morally and spiritually excellent, consecrated, and set apart. It is the quality of abhorring evil, unrighteousness, and anything that is polluted or unclean. Habakkuk 1:13 states that God is of purer eyes than to behold evil and cannot look upon injustice and wickedness. God cannot stand the sight of evil! He is holy, infinitely holy! "God's holiness is the all-consuming, purifying perfection that sanctifies and makes holy, anything that comes in contact with Him." (*Single and Happy*). In Isaiah 6:1-3, we see a glimpse of how holy God is. Isaiah saw a vision of God sitting on His throne, surrounded by His court. Attending Him were mighty Seraphim. These angels were constantly calling out to each other, "Holy, holy, holy is the Lord of Heaven's armies! The whole earth is filled with His glory!" "The cry of the Seraphim is not a scripted cry. It is an exclamation, a spontaneous reaction to the utter and indescribable holiness of Almighty God. It is their unvarnished response to what they behold, a God who is so absolutely, flawlessly holy!" (*Single and Happy*).

God has many supernatural attributes. He is love, He is light, He is the truth, He is righteous, and so on. Why is it, that of all the attributes of God, His holiness is the one attribute that provokes the alarmed cry of the heavenly beings? This is because God's holiness is not just one discreet attribute, but the totality of all of God's moral perfection and surpassing excellence put together. Holiness is God's total glory crowned!

> *Holiness is God's total glory crowned!*

God is Good: To be good is to be and do what is morally right; to be virtuous. God is infinitely good. But what does that mean - that God is good? Dr. David Jeremiah explains, "God's goodness conveys His generosity. His goodness means far more than His generosity, but it certainly includes His infinitely generous attitude towards us. By nature, He longs to bring joy and blessing to all His creatures."

God's goodness also denotes and showcases His majesty and glory. God is a great King, and one of the attributes of kingship is benevolence. The ability and capacity to do good for His people, is an attribute that adorns, and elevates the throne of any king, and endears the king to the people in His kingdom. In Exodus 33:18-19, when Moses asked to see God's glory, "The Lord replied, "I will make all my goodness pass before you, and I will call out my name, Yahweh, before you. For I will show mercy to anyone I choose, and I will show compassion to anyone I choose." This scripture highlights the goodness of God and makes clear that God's goodness is an integral aspect of His glory. When God did in fact pass in front of Moses in Exodus 34:6-7, He proclaimed of Himself, "The Lord, the Lord, the compassionate and gracious God, slow to anger, abounding in love and faithfulness, maintaining love to thousands, and forgiving wickedness, rebellion and sin." The one word summary of this proclamation is "good". God is good!

The Bible said of Jesus, that He went about doing good and healing all who were sick and oppressed by the devil (Acts 10:38). God's goodness is a major theme that is replete throughout the Bible. A common refrain in the Psalms and throughout much of the Old Testament is, "God is good, and His mercies endure forever". When Jesus was called "good teacher", He said, "Why do you call me good? No one is good except God only." (Luke 18:19). To illustrate, He explained that if we, human beings, imperfect as we are, know how to lovingly care for and give good gifts to our children, how much more will our heavenly Father give the best to us His children? (Matthew 7:11). The scriptures affirm that everything good and perfect is a gift from God. Here's the sum: The God of heaven is a good God, He is who He says that He is, and does exactly what He says that He will do.

> *We can believe in the goodness of God even when we don't understand all the details.*

One favorite strategy of the devil is to tempt us to doubt God's goodness. It is the age old question about good and evil. Why would a good God allow evil in the world? A couple years ago, I and a group of my friends went on street evangelism. We went to a local park and shared the gospel, one on one, with whoever would listen. I and my daughter spoke to a young man. He was very attentive and as we engaged him in conversation, it was clear that he was very educated and rational in his thought process. His one stumbling block was this very issue; how can a good God allow so much evil in the world? He logically posited that there was an irreconcilable conflict between God's goodness and his omnipotence. It's either God is not omnipotent and cannot stop the rampant evil in the world, or He is not good. He could not be both. This young man rejected the concept of man's free will and personal responsibility, in conjunction with the devil, for perpetrating evil in our world.

The truth is that God is not to blame for the evil in the world. One of my friends put it succinctly - man was made in the image of God and as such, was given free will. God gave man a lease to rule the earth. Unfortunately, man made the choice, with his free will, to turn that lease over to the devil, who has wreaked havoc on planet earth ever since.

> *The God of heaven is a good God, He is who He says that He is, and does exactly what He says that He will do.*

Human reasoning on the question of good and evil, and trying to understand every detail about God has derailed the faith of many Christians. Charles Templeton and Billy Graham were close friends who rose to fame as evangelists in the 1940s. In fact, Templeton was the one everybody thought would become a worldwide evangelist. However, he ended up leaving the Christian faith, and eventually became an atheist because of this and other unanswered questions about God. His need to fully understand, with human reasoning, all the details about infinite God, overrode his convictions and he died in 2001, at the age of 86, as an atheist. This is the devil's classic tactic. He perpetrates evil, and then he gets people to blame God for it! He wants you to let your circumstances define your God. But that is a recipe for disaster. God is good, period! We can believe in the goodness of God even when we don't understand all the details. Our response should be, "This situation is not good, but God, you are good!"

In 2018, I had an experience that crystalized in my mind precisely what the Bible means when it says that God is good. My daughter had an advanced reading course for the summer. One of the recommended books was "Things Fall Apart" By Chinua Achebe. First published in 1958, the book depicts pre-colonial life in the Southeastern part of Nigeria and the arrival of the Europeans during the late 19th century. I had read the book in high school and was terrified. So, when I saw it on my daughter's reading list, I decided to read it again, before she does. I wanted to evaluate it from an adult perspective, and be ready to answer any questions my daughter may have. The book described, in bone chilling detail, the practice of ancestral worship, and how these wicked spirits ruled the lives of the people with an iron fist of fear, retribution, and terror. Whole groups of people were deemed outcasts and untouchables; twin babies were left to die in the evil forest because twins were considered taboo; communities engaged in human sacrifice, even of their own kin, to appease these evil spirits; and yet, regardless of all their efforts, it was never enough. People lived in perpetual fear and terror of provoking the wrath of these evil spirits, and the harsh reprisal that would follow. After I read the book, I fell to my knees and thanked God for His goodness. The contrast between these malevolent spirits and the God of the Bible is stark. In every case, God intervened to rescue, heal, restore, and give honor, dignity and value to every person, including the outcasts and those condemned to death. Substitute Buddhism, Islam, Hinduism or any other religion for ancestral worship and the contrast is just as stark. The Christian God stands alone in His love, care, and goodness towards humanity. It became crystal clear to me what the Bible means when it says that God is good. He is intrinsically, innately, benevolent, loving and full of grace. He loves and tremendously values every human being, and wants what is best for them. God is good!

God is Light: God is light, pure light, and there is no trace of darkness in Him. He created light, and is Himself light. Light commands attention, exposes flaws, provides direction and overpowers darkness. God does exactly that! The Bible says that God lives in intense and unapproachable light (1 Timothy 6:16). First John 1:5-6 declares, "God is light and in Him is no darkness at all. If we say that we have fellowship with Him, and walk in darkness, we lie and do not practice the truth." In the book of Revelation, we learn that in heaven where God lives, there is no need for sun or moon, because God Himself is the everlasting light. In John's gospel, Jesus said of Himself, "I am the light of the world. He who follows Me shall not walk in darkness, but have the light of life." Then He turned around and said to us, "you are the light of the world, a city that is set on a hill cannot be hidden."

Here is the truth, God is light, and those who embrace Him will experience life-giving light, and by reason of that association, will not walk in darkness. They don't have to do anything to escape darkness, that is, anything more than coming to the light. Once light shines, darkness dissipates. John 1:5 makes this point when it states that light shines in the darkness, and darkness cannot overcome or extinguish it. What this means is that in any contest between light and darkness, light will win; light will overtake darkness, every single time. The closer we come to the light, the farther we move from darkness. It's as simple as that. We don't have to pray, fast, yell or even try; we simply need to move towards the light, and darkness will, by necessity, flee!

> Once light shines, darkness dissipates.

God is Love: God is love. The Bible says that in 1 John 4:8. Love is not what God does, it is who He is. Love is God's activating, motivating and organizing principle. It is the defining attribute of the Godhead that underlies everything He says and does. God's love is actionable compassion. The beloved Bible verse, John 3:16, states it so eloquently, "For God so loved the world that He gave His one and only Son, so that whoever believes in Him will not perish but have everlasting life." In 1 Corinthians 13, apostle Paul outlines how fundamental love is to the plan of redemption when he said that even if we give our bodies to be burned, without love, it will profit nothing. This means that the sacrifice of Jesus on the cross would have been empty and bereft of any power to save mankind if it was not originated, motivated and empowered by love. God loves in a way that no human can fathom. God loves completely, unconditionally and eternally. In Jeremiah 31:3, He says, "I have loved you with an everlasting love". Nobody else is capable of that kind or depth of love. Nothing can separate us from the love of God! Neither death nor life, neither angels nor demons, neither our fears for today nor our worries about tomorrow—not even the powers of hell, can separate us from God's love.

> *Love is God's activating, motivating and organizing principle. It is the defining attribute of the Godhead that underlies everything He says and does.*

God's love is unilateral and inexhaustible. In Ephesians 3, apostle Paul prayed that we would discover the great magnitude of God's astonishing love toward us in all its dimensions – the width, length, depth and height. His love is deeply intimate, enduring, far-reaching, and inclusive! It is endless, lavish beyond measure, and transcends our understanding. Paul's prayer is that this extravagant love will pour into us, fill us, and complete us until we overflow with the fullness of life and power that comes from God.

God's agape love is the theme of many a song, book, poem, painting and other works of art. But of all the many songs that chronicle God's love, the one that, in my view, fitly captures the rapturous wonder of His love is the 1917 hymn by Frederick M. Lehman. The lyrics move me every single time:

The Love of God

The love of God is greater far
Than tongue or pen can ever tell;
It goes beyond the highest star,
And reaches to the lowest hell;
The guilty pair, bowed down with care,
God gave His Son to win;
His erring child He reconciled,
And pardoned from his sin.

> *Refrain:*
> Oh, love of God, how rich and pure!
> How measureless and strong!
> It shall forevermore endure—
> The saints' and angels' song.

When hoary time shall pass away,
And earthly thrones and kingdoms fall,
When men who here refuse to pray,
On rocks and hills and mountains call,
God's love so sure, shall still endure,
All measureless and strong;
Redeeming grace to Adam's race—
The saints' and angels' song.

Could we with ink the ocean fill,
And were the skies of parchment made,
Were every stalk on earth a quill,
And every man a scribe by trade;
To write the love of God above
Would drain the ocean dry;
Nor could the scroll contain the whole,
Though stretched from sky to sky.

God is Gracious: Grace is the unmerited favor of God. It is courteous goodwill and kindness, unasked for and undeserved. It is the free, unearned, love, favor and blessing of God; the spring and source of all the benefits mankind receives from Him. Grace is the beneficial influence, help and providence of Almighty God. It is His favor toward the unworthy and His benevolence on the undeserving. Throughout the Bible, God is described as gracious and full of compassion, slow to anger and abounding in mercy and lovingkindness. John 1:17 says that, out of His abundance and fullness we have all received, all have a share and are all supplied with one grace after another, and spiritual blessing upon spiritual blessing, and favor upon favor, and gift heaped upon gift.

In the Old Testament, the word that is most often translated into Grace is the Hebrew word, *hen*, in the New Testament, it is the Greek word *Charis*. Grace first occurs in Genesis 6:8, where Noah finds "grace (favor) in the eyes of the Lord." In the New Testament, apostle Paul begins every letter with the greeting, "Grace to you and peace from God our Father and the Lord Jesus Christ", and ends each letter with a benediction of grace. Grace is a person; His name is Jesus.

> *Neither the passage of time, human failure, or the devil himself can stop the promise of God.*

To fully understand grace, we need to consider who we were without Christ and who we become with Christ. We were born in sin, enemies of God, alienated from the commonwealth of Israel, strangers to the covenant of promise, without hope and deserving of death. We were unrighteous, unholy, without God, or any means of salvation. Spiritually, we were destitute, blind, unclean, and dead. Our souls were in peril of eternal damnation and everlasting punishment. But then came grace! God extended His favor to us. The gospel is the good news of God's saving Grace. His grace gave us salvation, restoration, victory over sin, and the hope of eternal life. God adopted us into His family, gave us His name, His abiding presence, and His precious promises. He gave us the Holy Spirit to live in us, seal us, mark us indelibly as His children, and to teach us how to access and walk in His wonderful grace. He granted us unlimited access to his limitless resources; and a priceless inheritance, pure and undefiled; a perfect inheritance that can never perish, never tarnish, and never diminish; promised by God and preserved forever in heaven for us! Our only rightful response is "Thank You, Lord, for your grace too wonderful for words!"

God is Faithful: God is faithful, meaning that He acts with good faith. He keeps His promises, performs His word and executes His covenant. He is dependable, trustworthy, reliable and steadfast. He is blameless, without fault, of moral rectitude, and free from fraud, tricks, or subterfuge. God's faithfulness is a prominent theme throughout the Bible. In the Old Testament, God is described as the one who keeps covenant to a thousand generations, and the New Testament repeatedly declares His faithfulness. But God's faithfulness is not only proclaimed, it is put on display and demonstrated for all to see. In Genesis 3:15, God promised to send a Savior. That promise seemingly lay "dormant" for over a thousand years (Matthew 1:1-17). In this intervening period, was a multitude of human sin and failure; including incest, murder, adultery, and prostitution. But neither the passage of time, human failure, or the devil himself could stop the promise of God. When the right time came, God sent his Son, Jesus, to die for the sins of mankind, just as He promised. God always keeps His promises. He will keep His promises to you, no matter what.

God is Righteous: To be righteous means to be morally right, to be virtuous, to be good or excellent. To be free from guilt or sin, and to act in accordance with divine or moral law. It is safe to say that there is nothing that is more strongly declared in the Bible, than the righteousness of God. Ezra said, "O Lord God of Israel, you are righteous" (Ezra 9:15). And David intones, "Gracious is the Lord and righteous; yes, our God is merciful (Psalm 116:5).

What does the Bible mean when it says that God is righteous? Don Stewart explains: "This means that God's character or nature always leads Him to do that which is right. Righteousness is holiness in action. We can also refer to God's righteousness as God's justice." He reveals His righteousness by loving the things that are good and hating the things that are evil. God's righteousness demands and is revealed by both his reward and judgement. God will judge the unrighteous and reward the righteous. Romans 1:18 makes this clear. It states that "The wrath of God is revealed from heaven against all ungodliness and unrighteousness of men". In 2 Timothy 4:7-8, apostle Paul looking ahead to his departure from this life said, "I have fought the good fight, I have finished the race, I have kept the faith. Finally, there is laid up for me the crown of righteousness, which the Lord, the righteous Judge, will give to me on that day." God is a righteous judge who will judge the unrighteous and reward the righteous.

> *God's grace gave us salvation, restoration, victory over sin, and the hope of eternal life.*

Because God is righteous, He wants us, His children, to live righteously. In fact, our righteousness is both the fruit and evidence of our progeny. To this end, apostle John said, "When people do what is right, it shows that they are righteous, even as Christ is righteous. But when people keep on sinning, it shows that they belong to the devil, who has been sinning since the beginning. Those who have been born into God's family do not make a practice of sinning, because God's seed is in them" (1 John 3:7-9).

To empower us to *be* righteous, at our new birth, God recreated us in righteousness and true holiness, (Ephesians 4:22-24); to enable us to *live* righteously, He made us the righteousness of God in Christ (2 Corinthians 5:21); and to help us to *practice* righteousness, He daily credits faith to us as righteousness (Romans 4:22-24).

God is Immutable: This means that God does not mutate or change. He is the same yesterday, today and forever. In Malachi 3:6, He says of Himself, "I am the Lord, I change not". He does not grow old, lose any capability or diminish in any capacity or attribute. Throughout the Bible, God is described as the Rock to convey this attribute of unwavering stability, immovability and strength. In a world that is constantly sliding and shifting, it is such a glorious relief to know that our faith is built on the solid foundation of the immutability of God's person, character, and word. God cannot change (Malachi 3:6); God cannot lie (Titus 1:2); God does not vacillate and change His mind like human beings (Numbers 23:19). God can be safely trusted. He is all wise, almighty, omnipotent, omniscient, omnipresent, good, and faithful.

> *In a world that is constantly sliding and shifting, it is such a glorious relief to know that our faith is built on the solid foundation of the immutability of God's person, character, and word.*

Hebrews 6:13-18 captures the concept of God's immutability in accurate detail. It states, "When God made his promise to Abraham, since there was no one greater for him to swear by, he swore by himself, saying, "I will surely bless you and give you many descendants." And so, after waiting patiently, Abraham received what was promised. People swear by someone greater than themselves, and the oath confirms what is said and puts an end to all argument. Because God wanted to make the unchanging nature of his purpose very clear to the heirs of what was promised, he confirmed it with an oath. God did this so that, by two unchangeable things in which it is impossible for God to lie, his promise and his oath, we who have fled to take hold of the hope set before us may be greatly encouraged."

Here's the sum: God is infinite, eternal, omnipotent, omnipresent, omniscient, righteous, holy, loving, and gracious. He is unfathomable, uncontainable, unexplainable and indescribable. He obliterates the theory of evolution. He is the First Cause.

    The First Cause of limitless space must be infinite

    The First Cause of boundless energy must be omnipotent

    The First Cause of endless time must be eternal

    The First Cause of universal interrelationship must be omnipresent

    The First Cause of infinite complexity must be omniscient.

    The First Cause of moral values must be moral.

    The First Cause of spiritual values must be spiritual.

    The First Cause of human responsibility must be volitional.

    The First Cause of human love must be loving.

    The First Cause of life must be living! (*Arno*).

God Almighty is the First Cause, He is the First and Last, the Beginning and the End.

CHAPTER 10
GOD-SHAPED - THE DIVINE DNA IN US

God is our heavenly Father. That means that the divine seed or "sperm" of God is in us. Second Corinthians 5:17 states that, anyone who belongs to Christ has become a new creation; old things have passed away; and all things have become new. The new is the divine DNA. It is implanted into us at the new birth. We are re-created in the image of God, and all that was lost in Adam is restored to us. Our spirits are reimaged with the imprint of God's image, and we are infused with and come alive spiritually with the "Zoe" life of God; the abundant, victorious, eternal life of God. First John 3:9 makes clear that the transaction that takes place at salvation transmits to us the DNA of God. It states, "No one born of God deliberately, knowingly, and habitually practices sin, for God's nature abides in him, His principle of life, the divine sperm, remains permanently within him; and he cannot practice sinning because he is born of God." 1 John 3:9 AMPC.

> *Both the Holy Spirit and the Word give us entrance into the spirit realm, and the power to confront and overcome sin, the devil, the flesh and the world.*

The DNA of God inside us gives us:

1. Access to and authority in God's world, the supernatural!

2. The Holy Spirit and the Word of God to act as our

    "spiritual" or 6th sense and help us navigate the spiritual world, just as the 5 senses help us to navigate the physical world. Both the Holy Spirit and the Word give us entrance into the spirit realm, and the power to confront and overcome sin, the devil, the flesh and the world. Both the Holy Spirit and the Word are diametrically opposed to the dictates of our natural, physical, fleshly, desires (Galatians 7:17-18).

3. The ability to have and deploy the mind of Christ. We can think differently, with an elevated perspective. We can think like God (1 Corinthians 2:16). We can understand the mysteries of God, possess the thoughts and perceptions of Christ's mind, and implement His purposes on the earth.

4. Supernatural wisdom that transcends this world; the wisdom from above, which is pure, peace-loving, considerate, teachable, submissive, full of mercy and good fruit, never displays prejudice or hypocrisy, and sincere (James 3:17).

5. The creative ability of God. We can conceive and birth the plans and purposes of God. We can see through His eyes and speak through the power of His voice. We can speak as God speaks, calling into being things that don't yet exist, and creating new things out of nothing (Romans 4:17).

6. The capacity for holiness. We can be holy, as God is holy. Because God is so infinitely holy, and created us to have fellowship with Him, He knows that unholiness would, not only bar us from His presence, but would destroy us

altogether, hence His loving directive to us in Hebrews 12:14 to live a holy life.

In God's economy, everything reproduces after its kind. God made us like Himself, implanted His DNA in us, and commissioned us to reproduce after our kind. This is our mission on earth, to replicate the divine DNA. To accomplish this, God made us His representatives on the planet, delegated His authority to us, appointed us as His ambassadors to the world, and ordained us as ministers of reconciliation with the express mandate to call people back to God, invite them to receive His finished work of reconciliation and His free gift of salvation. Jesus' last words to His disciples underscored the urgency of this mission. He said, "Go into all the world and make disciples of all nations, baptizing them in the name of the Father and the Son and the Holy Spirit. Teach these new disciples to obey all the commands I have given you. And be sure of this: I am with you always, even to the end of the age" (Matthew 28:19-20). When we make disciples, we are replicating the divine DNA.

> *Our mission on earth is to replicate the divine DNA.*

Components of Our Spiritual Identity

The New Birth: This is how we acquire the divine DNA, by being born into God's family. At the new birth, God's Holy Spirit moves in and takes up residence in our hearts. He transmits the life of God and the divine DNA into us, and writes God's word on the tablet of our hearts. He gives us a purpose, relationship, and destiny based identity. We belong to God! Then He certifies us with the divine seal of authenticity and proceeds to testify and confirm to our spirit that we are indeed the children of God. (Romans 8:16). We become living epistles, God's love letters, written by Christ to the world, not with ink but by the Spirit of the living God.

> *We desperately need and cannot succeed in our Christian walk without the ministry of the Holy Spirit!*

The Holy Spirit: The Holy Spirit represents Christ, and acts on His behalf. He seals or marks the believer with the favor, protection, ownership and authority of God. He is the Comforter, Counselor, Helper, Intercessor, Advocate, Strengthener, and Standby. He is the heavenly power source resident on the earth today. It is He who energizes the will of God, giving it life and substance. When the Bible says in Philippians 2:13, that "God is working in you, giving you the desire and the power to do what pleases him", it is talking about the Holy Spirit. He is the One who breathes God's life into any situation. He teaches believers, gives us power to be witnesses for Christ, maintains fellowship with us, and facilitates our fellowship with the Father and the Son. He helps us in our weaknesses - areas where we are prone to sin, failure, deficiency or inadequacy. He also equips us for service, and helps us to administer the resources, plans, and agenda of God. We desperately need and cannot succeed in our Christian walk without the ministry of the Holy Spirit! His work is to help us to become who we are, sons and daughters of Almighty God! (*Choosing A Life of Victory*).

The Word of God: The word of God is the seed of God. It is the divine sperm that contains the DNA of God. The word of God is powerful! It is the supernatural mold and frame for human transformation First Peter 1:23 states that we are born again not from a mortal seed or sperm, but the incorruptible, immortal, ever living and lasting word of God, and this seed that He planted within us can never be destroyed but will live and grow inside us forever. When angel Gabriel visited Mary and told her that she would give birth to the Christ Child, she was impregnated with the word or seed of God. This is because the word of God is God Himself. John 1:1 makes that clear. The word of God implanted and rooted in our lives, contains the power to save our souls and change us into the image of Christ from the inside, out. It is living and active, sharper than any two-edged sword, with unparalleled precision to slice between the soul and spirit, and to discern our innermost thoughts and desires. The word of God is the mirror of the spirit. It shows me who I am, how I look, what I have, and what I can be. It describes my spirit. The word of God is eternal. It is backed by the person and character of God.

> *The word of God is the mirror of the spirit. It shows me who I am, how I look, what I have, and what I can be.*

Obedience to God: Obedience to God and His word is the clearest evidence of the divine DNA in a believer. It is the unalloyed, unmitigated proof of your love for and commitment to Christ. Jesus said, if you love me, keep my commandments. It's as simple as that! Apostle James, in his practical, no nonsense way, said, "be doers of the word and not hearers only, deceiving ourselves". What Jesus and His half-brother James are saying is, the hard core evidence that you love God, is not how many scriptures you memorize, how much you serve at church, fast and pray, or work for God, but whether you live obediently and apply the word of God in your daily life. Obedience to God starts with changing your thoughts to line up with the thoughts of God. Romans 12:2 calls this process renewing your mind, and gives us the recipe. It says, "Don't copy the behavior and customs of this world, but let God transform you into a new person by changing the way you think. Then you will learn to know God's will for you, which is good and pleasing and perfect." "Renewing your mind means that once you find out what the Bible says, you believe it as truth, and if your own thoughts on an issue are different or inconsistent with what the Bible says, you set aside your thoughts, and replace them with what the Bible says" (*Single and Happy*).

Relationship with God: God created us for relationship, and our daily, consistent, fellowship with God is evidence of our deep roots and ongoing growth in Christ. Regular fellowship cultivates the presence of God and hones our ability to hear and recognize His voice. God created us for companionship with Himself. When He made Adam, there was no soul to save, no world to serve, no sickness to heal, and none hungry to feed. He simply hung out with Adam in the evening and fellowshipped with him. Because we are made in the image and likeness of God, human beings have the ability to know God, so we can love Him, worship Him, serve Him and fellowship with Him. Jesus came to give us understanding, so that we can know God as our Father and live in fellowship with him. Simply stated, God created us for His pleasure, because He delights in us.

Biblical Worldview: Worldview is the lens through which you view the world. If you wear blue sunglasses, everything you see will be tinted blue. Same thing with your worldview, it colors everything you see. Everyone has a worldview, the question is, what kind is it? Your worldview can be secular, ideological, political or biblical. We would expect that a Christian would have a biblical world view, but sadly, this is not always the case. Due to apathy, ignorance of the word of God, the new world religion of "tolerance" and a false definition of "love and peace", many Christians either do not possess or have relinquished or traded in their biblical values and worldview for a secular one.

God created us for companionship with Himself.

Research released in 2020 by the Barna Group on the state of the church, chronicles the shocking decline in biblical worldview among evangelical Christians. It found that 52% of evangelical Christians in America believe that there is no absolute moral truth; 58% believe that the Holy Spirit is merely symbolic; 40% believe that sex between unmarried people is okay; 40% believe that lying is not viewed as sinful behavior anymore; 44% believe that the Bible does not take a stand on abortion; only 36% seek to pursue God's will for their lives; 42% seek moral guidance from sources other than the Bible; and 34% believe that homosexual marriage is okay. American Christians have made a God in their own image!

This data is woeful, and shows a sad departure from the clear teachings of the Bible. This belief system does not represent a biblical worldview. To turn America back to its godly principles, and its Judeo Christian foundations, we must go back to the Bible.

CHAPTER 11
PROOF OF IDENTITY

Man is a spirit, who has a soul, and lives in a body. When a person is born again, they are "blessed with every spiritual blessing in the heavenly realms" (Ephesians 1:3). This means that the life, identity, and limitless resources of Almighty God are deposited in their spirit. These abundant and lavish resources are very real, but they exist in the spirit world. The soul is the conduit between the spirit world and the physical world. To access these resources already provided by God, they must align their soul with their spirit. This opens "the valve" and allows God's resources to flow unhindered from their spirit, through their soul, into the physical realm.

Most people can describe themselves, at least 2/3rd of themselves. No one has ever really "seen" themselves, but we have seen reflections of ourselves in a mirror; and can accurately describe how we look physically, our height, weight and facial features. Most of us can also describe our soul space with a high degree of accuracy. We can describe our emotional, mental, and social capability and characteristics. Another word for this is personality. We know ourselves and can describe our personality fairly well. But most people cannot describe their spirit, which is the real person. Where do you go to find out how you look in the spirit? In the word of God! In John 6:63, Jesus said that His words are spirit and life. And James 1:23-25 states that the word of God is a mirror that shows us how we look in the spirit. God's word illuminates our spirits, floods our hearts with light, and enables us to see ourselves the way God sees us. So, to accurately describe your spirit man, you need to look through the lens of the word of God. It tells you who you are, how you look, and what you have in the spirit.

Who Are You?

> *Where do you go to find out how you look in the spirit? In the word of God!*

The simple question, "Who Are You?" can elicit vastly different answers from different people based on their self-definition. Consider yourself, for example. What is the first thing that comes to mind when you hear that question? Is it your occupation, gender, race, ethnicity or political affiliation? Your response is critical, both in substance and sequence, because whatever your identity, that is what you are empowered to become.

For those who identify themselves by their position. Their response to the question would be: I AM a nurse, doctor, manager, mom, dad, wife, and so on. This is a status driven identity. The problem is; who are you, when you are not or no longer a doctor, nurse, husband or wife? Others identify themselves by their performance, and accomplishments. This is an achievement driven identity. These people gather a lot of trophies as they walk through life, because this is how they justify their existence and get their sense of self-worth. But they lose themselves and fall to pieces when they can no longer achieve, because they confuse their "who" with their "do".

Others identify themselves by their possessions and how much money they have. This is a wealth driven identity. Sadly, these people sacrifice what is most important in life, and sometimes their eternal souls to acquire material possessions, only to find that they are emptier than ever. They discover, too late, that money makes a lot of promises that it cannot keep. Some others identify themselves by their popularity, public recognition, fame and human approval. This is a crowd or people driven identity. This is particularly prevalent in today's social media world. Unfortunately, it is probably the most fragile foundation to base your identity on because people are fickle, and their approval is transient at best. In trying to please the crowd, these people compromise themselves and lose their personal moorings. When the inevitable human rejection, spurn, and about face occurs, it is often too much to bear and they self-destruct.

> *Whatever your identity, that is what you are empowered to become.*

"Who are you?" is a question we must all be prepared to answer. It is a question about identity, self-awareness and self-definition. It is a question about your personal mandate and authority. It is also a question about self-image, and how you see yourself in Christ.

In Acts 19:13-16, the Bible tells the story of seven young men whose failure to answer this question cost them dearly.

> A group of Jews was traveling from town to town casting out evil spirits. They tried to use the name of the Lord Jesus in their incantation, saying, "I command you in the name of Jesus, whom Paul preaches, to come out!" Seven sons of Sceva, a leading priest, were doing this. But one time when they tried it, the evil spirit replied, "I know Jesus, and I know

Paul, but who are you?" Then the man with the evil spirit leaped on them, overpowered them, and attacked them with such violence that they fled from the house, naked and battered.

In this account, we see why it is dangerous to operate as a Christian without having your identity rooted in Christ. It is like operating a car without a license or going to withdraw money from a bank without proof of identity. These young men had probably seen apostle Paul cast out evil spirits in the name of Jesus, and thought, "How cool! We can do that too." They figured that being the sons of a chief priest qualified them or at least gave them the authentication to do the same thing. But they were sadly mistaken. Their mistake became apparent when the evil spirit asked them, "who are you?" and they had no legitimate response.

By contrast, let's look at the two men who were referenced by the sons of Sceva in that scripture. Jesus and apostle Paul. Jesus was asked that same question by the devil himself. Matthew 4:3 records the incident:

> Jesus was led by the Spirit into the wilderness to be tempted there by the devil. For forty days and forty nights he fasted and became very hungry. During that time the devil came and said to him, "If you are the Son of God, tell these stones to become loaves of bread."

"If you are the son of God" is the devil's challenge to the identity and authority of Christ. Jesus's response was immediate and

unequivocal. His response was from the word of God. He said, "The Scriptures say, 'People do not live by bread alone, but by every word that comes from the mouth of God.'" He pointed to the scriptures as the source of truth, authority and identity. These same scriptures clearly identify Him as the Son of God. When the devil persisted, Jesus exercised His authority to rebuke and banish the devil. He said, "Get out of here, Satan".

Apostle Paul answered that question as well. He wrote about half of the New Testament, and he began each letter with this identification, "This letter is from Paul, chosen by the will of God to be an apostle of Jesus Christ". And in Galatians 2:20, he boldly declared, "My old self has been crucified with Christ. It is no longer I who live, but Christ lives in me." Paul clearly knew who he was, and like Jesus, he drew his identity, personal authority and apostolic mandate from the word of God and his relationship with Christ.

John the Baptist confronted that question too. The Jewish leaders sent an entourage of priests and temple servants to interrogate John, and they asked him, "Who are you?" John answered, "I am not the Messiah!" "Then who are you?" they asked. "Are you Elijah?" "No," John replied. "Are you the prophet Moses said was coming?" "No," he replied. "Then who are you?" they demanded. John responded with the words of the prophet Isaiah, "I am the voice in the wilderness saying prepare the way of the Lord" (John 1:19-22).

Here again, we see the same dynamic at play. John knew exactly who he was and like Jesus and Paul, he drew his self-definition, proof of identity, and prophetic mandate directly from the word of

God; and would not submit to pressure to do otherwise. Later, we'll see how this self-definition protected him from temptation.

By contrast, the seven sons of Sceva had no direct relationship, first-hand knowledge, divine mandate or personal authority with, of, or from Christ or His word. All they had was hearsay evidence, which proved as useless in this instance, as it does in a court of law. They tried to use the authority of the name of Jesus by second hand association or like a magic wand. They did not know that the authority in the name comes from relationship and identification with God and His word. Someone has said that God does not have grandchildren. This shows that He does not go by the "buddy system" either.

> *The authority in the name of Jesus comes from relationship and identification with God and His word.*

The Devil Knows

Did you notice that the evil spirits also referenced Jesus and Paul? They knew who they were! Now, the Bible makes clear that God knows those who are His. Romans 8:15-16, states that God adopted us into His family, that He is our "Abba" or daddy, and that the Holy Spirit bears witness with our spirit that we are God's children. He also seals us with His divine signet ring or imprint that identifies us as belonging to God.

Second Timothy 2:19 confirms this truth and sets a criterion. It states that our relationship with God is built on and evidenced by a solid foundation inscribed with this seal, "Let everyone who names the name of Christ depart from iniquity." Therein lies the litmus test for those who belong to Christ – abstain from evil. This identity marker is replete throughout scripture. First John 3:9-10 puts it succinctly:

> Those who have been born into God's family do not make a practice of sinning, because God's seed is in them. So they can't keep on sinning, because they are children of God. So now we can tell who are children of God and who are children of the devil. Anyone who does not live righteously and does not love other believers does not belong to God.

This is why it is not sufficient identity to know that God exists, to believe in Him or to quote scripture. That is not enough! How do I know that? Because the devil does all three – he knows that God exists, he believes in God, he quotes the bible, and he even does more than that, he trembles (James 2:19). Yet that does not qualify him. Your identity must be rooted in a personal relationship with Christ.

> *The devil knows your true identity. He knows those who belong to God, not because of what they say, but because of whose insignia they bear and the life they live.*

The devil knows your true identity. He knows those who belong to God, not because of what they say, but because of whose insignia they bear and the life they live. In Philippi, Paul and Silas were trailed by a slave girl with a demonic spirit of divination. She followed them around shouting, "These men are servants of the

Most High God, and they have come to tell you how to be saved." Imagine that, being announced by the devil! Jesus had several encounters with evil spirits who recognized him right away. In one such encounter recorded in Mark 1:24, the evil spirit cried out, "What do you want with us, Jesus of Nazareth? Have you come to destroy us? I know who you are – the Holy One of God!" Make no mistake, the devil knows when you are operating with proof of identity and when you are not.

Who Do You Say That I Am?

Jesus prepared His disciples to answer this same question. In Matthew 16:13-20, He asked them, "Who do men say that I am?" And after they reported hearsay evidence, Jesus made it personal! He asked pointedly, "But who do YOU say I am?" Peter's inspired response, "You are the Christ, the Son of the living God" was a powerful proof and declaration of identity, not only for Jesus, but for Peter:

1. It came from a place of knowledge and relationship. It's been a couple years since that fateful day when Jesus called Peter to become a "fisher of men". He and the other disciples had since walked and lived with Jesus daily. Usually, close proximity and personal knowledge tends to diminish awe and reverence. This reality is reflected in the common adage, "familiarity breeds contempt." But not in the case of Christ. Their familiarity with Him provided powerful confirmation of His authenticity and divinity.

2. This level of spiritual insight came from revelation. Only God could have revealed this to Peter. Peter's response showed that he not only had knowledge of who Jesus was by experience, but he also knew Him by revelation.

3. This revelation gave Peter personal authority and a powerful mandate. Jesus said, "Now I say to you that you are Peter, and upon this rock I will build my church and all the powers of hell will not conquer it." Personal and revelatory knowledge of Christ provided a powerful authentication, identity and validation for Peter that will stop the advance of and vanquish all the powers of hell.

Only those with this intimate relationship and personal mandate can receive and exercise the incredible grant of authority that followed. Jesus said to Peter, "And I will give you the keys of the kingdom of Heaven. Whatever you bind on earth will be bound in heaven, and whatever you loose on earth, will be loosed in heaven." Wow! This is the same authority that Paul had and exercised to cast out devils. The sons of Sceva saw the demonstration, manifestation and exercise of this authority, but did not know the source, root or origin. They liked the power that Paul had, but did not want to do what he did to get it. Well, the demon taught them a lesson they will not soon forget, in the spirit realm, you must have proof of identity!

> *"Who are you?" Is a question we must all be prepared to answer.*

Who Wants to Know?

It's not only the devil, his demons and agents who want to know who you are. Your circumstances, the giants and mountains in your life; and your emotions are all asking or will ask you the question, "who are you?". Sickness will ask you that question. Relationship problems will ask you that question. Failure and poverty will ask you that question. Success will also ask you that question. They all want to know who you are. They are in fact challenging your identity, and forcing you to declare and enforce it.

To accurately respond, you must operate from the realm of your spirit, and be in relationship and daily fellowship with the Lord Jesus. That foundation provides the solid platform, and gives you the sure footing to authoritatively engage the devil and his agents and win, just like Jesus and Paul did.

CHAPTER 12
YOUR IDENTITY WILL BE CHALLENGED

Your identity will be challenged, guaranteed! The devil will challenge your identity, the same way he challenged Jesus. In Matthew 4:3, he said to Jesus, "If you are the son of God, tell these stones to become loaves of bread." Keep in mind that this was right after Jesus had been publicly declared to be the Son of God. After His baptism, as He came up out of the water, the heavens were opened, the Holy Spirit descended like a dove and settled on Him, and God the Father proclaimed in a loud voice from heaven "This is my beloved Son, in whom I am well pleased" (Matthew 3:16–17).

This is the one time in scripture when the entire Godhead—the Father, the Son, and the Holy Spirit congregated in the earth, in one place, at one time, for one single purpose, to publicly confirm and affirm the identity and sonship of Christ. But that did not stop the devil! Right after that, he challenged Jesus's identity. But Jesus knew who He was and quickly put the devil in His place. He did not make it about Himself. He made it all about God and His Word. He did not need to prove Himself to the devil, or show off in pride. He is the Son of God. He knew that and walked in that authority without a flinch.

This is where the first Adam, and his wife, Eve, failed. Luke 3:38 tells us that Adam was "the son of God". But, sure enough, the devil challenged his identity and that of his wife Eve. When Eve told the devil about God's direction not to eat the fruit from the tree of the knowledge of good and evil, he said to her, "You won't die! God knows that your eyes will be opened as soon as you eat it, and you will be like God." Adam and Eve were already like God. They were made in His image! They were "sons" of God! But, they didn't know their identity and therefore did not exercise their authority to shut down the devil. He played to their pride, and they fell for his trick. As a result, they were seduced into disobeying God, and in so doing, lost their authority to the devil.

Identity is critical! This is why David was able to kill Goliath, when the trained soldiers could not. Goliath's challenge was really an identity challenge targeted to the men of war, the men who defined themselves by their military prowess, experience, and success. And for those men his strategy worked. However, David was different. He was not a man of war, at that time. He did not even have a spear or sword! When Saul gave David his own armor, a bronze helmet and a coat of mail, David put it on, took one step and said, "I can't go in these," "I'm not used to them" and he took them off. The normal war apparatus and infrastructure were absolutely ineffective for David. He was just a shepherd boy sent on an errand.

But in 1 Samuel 17: 45-47, David revealed the secret of his success. In those three verses, he mentioned the Lord eight times! He did not focus on the size of Goliath. His entire focus was on God and His mighty power. If he had engaged Goliath on his terms, he would have lost. But he retreated into God, and answered Goliath's identity challenge from that place of strength. He saw things the way they really looked in the spirit realm. And it was an unequal match, but not in the way Goliath envisaged, because the match was not David vs Goliath, but Goliath vs Almighty God!

Numbers 13:17-20 tells the heart breaking story of when God directed Moses to select twelve men to spy out the land of Canaan. For hundreds of years, the Israelites had prayed, hoped and dreamed of this day. Now, they are literally looking at the land God promised their fore fathers. Spying out this land was a very important assignment, so, Moses didn't just choose anybody. He handpicked a select group of men, all leaders of their tribes. These guys were the A Team; men whose opinions mattered; men of stature.

Before getting to this point, they had already seen God do many miracles. They had watched the ten plagues decimate the nation of Egypt and its people. They saw how God protected them in Goshen from all the plagues, and filled the Egyptians with fear at the power of Israel's God. They had seen God pay them massive reparations for years of slavery and transfer the wealth of Egypt to them. They had seen God open up the red sea before them, and drown Pharaoh and his army behind them. They had seen God provide manna and quail for them in the wilderness and bring water out of the rock.

> *God wants us to walk in the same authority that Jesus demonstrated in Matthew 4.*

All that notwithstanding, they allowed fear to seize their imaginations. Instead of doing what David did, and measuring their enemies against the size of their God, ten of the spies measured themselves against the size of their enemies. They played and replayed horror images in their minds of their own death and destruction. The more they thought about it, the more their enemies grew in size and they shrank, until they felt like grasshoppers, and their enemies looked like giants. Were they grasshoppers? No, not at all, but that is how they felt, and tragically, that is how they spoke. They said:

"We are not able to go up against the people, for they are stronger than we are" "The land through which we have gone as spies is a land that devours its inhabitants, and all the people whom we saw in it are men of great stature. There we saw the giants, and we were like grasshoppers in our own sight, and so we were in their sight."

God was not mentioned even once! By contrast, two of the spies, Joshua and Caleb, brought God into the fray and when they did, the situation shrank in size. While the ten spies spoke their feelings and fears, Joshua and Caleb spoke the word of God. They said, "if the LORD delights in us, then He will bring us into this land and give it to us, 'a land which flows with milk and honey.' Only do not rebel against the LORD, nor fear the people of the land, for they *are* our bread; their protection has departed from them, and the LORD is with us. Do not fear them."

> *Your identity and self-definition are critical to winning any battle.*

Like David, Joshua and Caleb trusted in the character of God, and they not only survived, when the other ten spies were destroyed in the wilderness; they lived to fight those giants, defeat them, and possess their inheritance, just as God had promised.

Your identity and self-definition are critical to winning any battle. God said, my people perish for lack of knowledge – knowledge of who they are in Christ. If you don't know your God or who you are in Him, when your identity is challenged, you will have an identity crisis and lose your way like Adam and Eve did. God wants us to walk in the same authority that Jesus demonstrated in Matthew 4. To do that, we must know, not only who we are, but whose we are. Do you know whose you are? If you do, then you can stand your ground and instruct the devil and his principalities and powers of their defeat and your victory in Christ. You can tell them about Colossians 2:13–15 which tells the tale of how Jesus disarmed and shamed them publicly. The Bible is clear, "the people that know their God, shall be strong and do exploits" (Daniel 11:32). If you know your God and who you are in Him, you shall be strong in the face of any challenge, and you shall do great exploits in His name.

CHAPTER 13
YOUR IDENTITY IN CHRIST

Having your identity in Christ is drawing your sense of self from your connection to and relationship with Christ. It is accepting the word of God and what it says about you as the absolute truth and final authority in your life, elevating that reality above all other sources of self-definition, and accepting it as your core foundation, against which every other definition is measured. Any other identity, label or description that is inconsistent with who Christ says you are is invalid, null, and void to the extent of their inconsistency with the word of God. Having your identity in Christ means that any other identity you hyphenate after Christ is idolatry, whether it is your ethnicity, race, profession, status, or political affiliation.

When your identity is in Christ, then the sum total of how you see, perceive, think of, speak of and present yourself is based solely and entirely on Christ and His word. Your identity in Christ is holding up the mirror of the Spirit, which is the word of God, looking deep into it, seeing your reflection, believing what you see without question, doubt, or hesitation, and acting on what you see with confidence, regardless of any contrary information from any other source! Having your identity in Christ is what Martin Luther meant by Solo Scriptura and Solo Christo. Christ and His word alone!

> *"Christ identity" is drawing your sense of self from your connection to and relationship with Christ.*

Marks of New Covenant Sonship

There are two key marks of new covenant sonship:

1. **Identity:** This gives you the right, authority and sense of belonging. In the natural world, your identity comes from your father. He determines your gender and gives you his last name, as a mark of ownership and belonging. You belong to his family! Likewise, spiritually, our identity comes from our heavenly Father. John 1:12 states, "But as many as received Him, to them he gave the power to become the sons of God, even to them that believe on His name." God gives us His name and identity to confirm that we are His. We belong to His family!

2. **Equality:** Our identity as children of God, gives us equality with Christ and access to the limitless resources and inheritance of our Father, God. Romans 8:17 states, "And if sons, then heirs—heirs of God and joint heirs with Christ." Because of this critical connection, a loss of identity, results in a loss of equality, and shuts down our access to the resources and inheritance of the Father.

When you know your identity, you are secure in the validation of your Heavenly Father and can confidently partake in your inheritance. On the other hand, if you do not know your identity, the devil can rob you of your inheritance as a child of God.

Who You Are in Christ

Christ has reconciled you to God, so, you have right standing with Him. Your body is the temple of the Holy Spirit who lives in you, and produces the fruit of love, joy, peace, patience, kindness, goodness, faithfulness, gentleness, and self-control. You are the head and not the tail, always on top and never at the bottom. You are the light of the world, and the salt of the earth. You are a shining city on a hill. You are blessed, chosen, forgiven, adopted, accepted, and justified in Christ. You are compassionate, humble, kind, meek and patient. You are forgiven of all your sins and made clean through the precious blood of Christ. You have been rescued from the domain and power of darkness, and brought into God's kingdom. You are redeemed from the curse of sin, sickness, poverty, and death. You are healed and made whole in Christ. You are saved by God's grace, raised up with Christ, and seated with Him in heavenly places. You are loved by God with an everlasting love. You have victory over fear because the Holy Spirit lives in you and gives you His power, love and self-control. You are a son or daughter of Almighty God!

For a Christian, knowledge of your identity in Christ is foundational to living the Christian life.

Why is Identity So Important?

Identity affects how you perceive and present yourself, and how others appraise and regard you. You interact with the world from the frame of your identity, and it impacts how you view and engage the world around you. Having a strong sense of identity provides a grounding, and gives you personal security, self-assurance and confidence. Identity also helps us to make decisions and know how to behave. People tend to conform their behavior to who they believe themselves to be.

For a Christian, knowledge of your identity in Christ is foundational to living the Christian life. It transcends all learning, prayer, sharing, studying, or serving at church. Knowing who you are in Christ attacks and demolishes fear, shame, self-doubt and lack of purpose. It establishes a personal baseline that enables you to rise like the phoenix, regardless of how many times you stumble. Knowing your identity in Christ is of incalculable value in ensuring stability and victory in your Christian walk.

Transactional Identity

In our transactional world, identity is of critical importance. It is at the core of every interaction of human beings, companies, organizations, and even devices. There are different components and implications of transactional identity, such as, what characteristics or attributes can be used to identify an entity, how to prove and validate them over time, when and with whom to share them, and what a person can do with those established identities.

Establishing your identity gives you several benefits:
1. **Recognition:** Identity confers recognition. For example, an online identity, such as a Facebook profile with your unique personal details gives you recognition. Neither Facebook as an organization or its founder, Mark Zuckerberg, know you personally. However, they have gathered certain details

about you that is unique to you. You can share some of those same details with others, such as a similar first or last name, but the overall combination of all those details uniquely identify only you. So, you could have two people with the same first name, but they may not have the same last name, or birth dates. If, for example, your name is John Smith, when you log on to Facebook and enter your log in details, the Facebook software executes a complex algorithm to recognize and distinguish you from all the other John Smiths on Facebook.

2. **Access:** Your identity is a key that opens some doors and closes others. Identity provides access. Once the software recognizes and identifies you, you are granted access to the online world of Facebook. You can go to your own page, post your photos, announce your events, host online parties, stream live, and so on, all for free! All these benefits flow from establishing your identity.

3. **Common Ground:** The recognition and access provided by a valid identity allows you to establish common ground and connect with other Facebook Users. You can "friend" people, send them birthday wishes, invite them to your events, and even send them money. You can create an online community of people who share your interests, status, affiliations or hobbies, or become part of a group or other community of like-minded people.

If you want a higher level of engagement on Facebook, for example, if you own a business and want to advertise and grow your business using Facebook, then a higher level of proof of identity and personal authentication is required. At the social connection level of engagement, you create and manage your profile. You can use fake names, fake date of birth, no address, or fake address. Facebook allows you to call yourself whatever you want and post whatever photo of "yourself" you like, as long as it is not inappropriate. However, when you begin to engage at a business owner level, ensuring your identity becomes financially important and additional layers of security are needed and applied. Also, this level of engagement comes at a cost. Facebook would require:

4. **Verification:** They want to verify that you are indeed who you present yourself to be. They require very detailed, personally identifiable and security information like your social security number or your business Employer Identification Number. They need to verify that the specific identity attributes you claim and present, like your name and address, are actually yours.

5. **Authentication:** At the authentication level, Facebook wants you to demonstrate not only that you are you, but that you and your business are legitimate. In fact, they want independent confirmation of your legitimacy. They want to be able to go back in time and validate that you can demonstrate ownership and control of the identity you claimed over time.

6. **Authorization:** To continue with our Facebook analogy, if you are successful in the verification and authentication process, then Facebook will authorize you to transact business on their platform. Even then, they have several layers of play with thresholds that escalate with the growth of your business. As you do more business, these validation requirements continue, and increase; but with each level comes more privileges, resources, and support.

7. **Federation:** This is when you can convey identity attributes, authentication and authorization across multiple parties or platforms. This is when you can use your Facebook profile to sign up on other online platforms without the need to establish your identity with them. Because Facebook has validated you, that gives you online "credibility" and other platforms can allow you to deploy your Facebook account on their platforms without further rigor or investigation.

Transactional Identity in The Kingdom

Unlike the world, God gives us the highest form of security clearance as soon as we become His children. This high level clearance comes directly from our Heavenly Father and is conferred upon us immediately upon our salvation and adoption into His family. We are duly authorized to rule and represent God, and have authority in three realms, in heaven, on the earth and under the earth. Access flows from that divine bequest, and we gain admission into the abundant resources of God. God knew us in our mother's wombs, so He does not need us to prove ourselves, perform, or present our qualifications or credentials. All we need is to show that we have been washed in the blood of the lamb and we are fully qualified to transact in the spirit!

Verification: When we become born again, the Holy Spirit joins with our spirit to verify that we are indeed God's children (Romans 8:16). Nobody comes to God, without the agency of the Holy Spirit (John 6:44). So, our verification comes from the highest quarters. Unlike the online world where we can create fake identities, the spiritual world is different. Nothing in all creation is hidden from God. Everything is naked and exposed before His eyes. (Hebrews 4:13). So, in the spirit world, our identity is clearly visible. The Holy Spirit does the work of confirmation and verification, and his work is complete, thorough and entire.

> *In the spirit world, your identity is clearly visible.*

Authentication: When we believe in Christ, He identifies us as His own and proceeds to put His seal or mark of authenticity upon us (Ephesians 1:13). The indwelling Holy Spirit is God's preserving seal to lock in our identity, and keep out destructive forces. This is a mark of ownership, belonging and security. Rick Renner explains, "In Greek and Roman times — and in certain places still today — if a package was to be dispatched to another location, it *FIRST* went through a series of investigations to make sure the contents were not flawed, broken, or shattered. If everything was whole and intact, the sender would pour hot wax on the crease of the package and then carefully push the insignia of the owner into the wax, signifying that all the contents were in perfect order. That "seal" was called a Sphragidzo — the exact same word used in Ephesians 1:13, where the Bible says we were "sealed" with the Holy Spirit when we believed in the Lord Jesus Christ." This insignia or seal on the package was important for several reasons. It was the sign of ownership and authenticity, as well as the guarantee that the package would be delivered to its final destination; and that everything in the package is in order — nothing missing, broken, inferior, or shattered. Everything was whole, complete, secure and tamper proof.

When we believed in Christ and became born again, God examined us thoroughly and found no flaws or defects. Colossians 1:22 states that He inspected us and certified us as holy, blameless, irreprovable, and without a single fault in His sight. God confirmed that we were truly a replica of Christ in the spirit and complete in Him. Then figuratively speaking, He poured His "wax" onto our hearts and spirits, and pressed His insignia, His image into us. He then put the Holy Spirit inside us, as guaranteed proof that we belong to Him and will make it to our final destination, heaven.

This divine seal preserves your spirit from the corruption and decay that is in the world. This means that when you sin as a Christian, the sin may enter into and corrupt your mind and body, and could give Satan an inroad into your life in those areas, but it cannot penetrate the seal around your spirit. You retain your sonship and right standing with God, no matter what. Your spirit is sealed, vacuum packed by the Holy Spirit, and eternally preserved in that perfect state forever!

> *When you sin as a Christian, the sin may enter into and corrupt your mind and body, but it cannot penetrate the seal around your spirit.*

Authorization: With verification and authentication comes authorization! In Luke 10:19, Jesus said, "Behold, I give you power and authority to tread on serpents and scorpions and on all the power of the devil and nothing shall by any means hurt you". Jesus clearly delegated His authority to us. He gave us His power and the authority to use it. The Greek words used for power and authority are the words: "Dunamis" – the ability or force to make possible, and "Exousia" – privilege, authority, capacity, and jurisdiction. It's like a police officer who is given the power and authority to administer justice. The badge is his authority, his Exousia; but the gun, taser, hand cuffs, car and training on how to apprehend criminals, are his Dunamis.

Same thing with us, Jesus gave us the jurisdiction, badge and authority to oversee and enforce His will in the earth. We have His authority, the name of Jesus, and the power of attorney to use His name, that is Exousia. We also have the Holy Spirit, His gifts, the word of God, and the power of God to enforce His will on earth, that is Dunamis.

Federation: Our identity and authorization in Christ is valid, recognized and instantly deployed across all spiritual platforms. The Bible says that upon our salvation, we are relocated in the spirit; translated from the kingdom of darkness into the kingdom of Christ (Colossians 1:13). We are seated in heavenly places in Christ, and our identity attributes, validation, authentication and authorization are conveyed across three realms, the heavens, the earth, and under the earth. Our names are written in the Lamb's book of life and we can transact kingdom business in Christ's name. This means that the new Christian has as much authorization and power as the mature Christian, the only difference is that he doesn't know it yet.

Access: Our identity as children of God gives us access to all of God's resources. It is the key that opens the door to heaven's store house. Jesus is a package deal. The same package that delivered our salvation, also included our healing, financial provision, favor, and more. Everything we need to live a godly life comes in our salvation package (2 Peter 1:3). In fact, the Greek word translated as "salvation" in the Bible is the word "Sozo" and that word means to save, deliver, make whole, restore, and heal. This means that when we gave our lives to Christ, we received the divine salvation package, which gave us access to heaven's store house and limitless resources.

Recognition: As the Holy Spirit works in us to produce the life of God in and through us, people can recognize us as God's Children. We begin to change from the inside out as we are conformed to the image of Christ. As we are progressively transformed, people will see our outward behavior, and recognize the change in us.

> *Jesus is a package deal. The same package that delivered our salvation, also included our healing, financial provision, favor, and everything we need to live a godly life on earth.*

Common Ground: As we grow, we begin to identity with our new family, the family of God. We see ourselves and others through the eyes of God, find affinity and common ground with other Christians and form or join communities of faith. We find a sense of belonging that transcends race, gender, language and any other identities. This is why you can travel to any city in the world, step into a church service, and immediately recognize that you are with your spiritual family! As long as it is a Bible believing church where the Holy Spirit leads, when you walk in, you will immediately synch with the other believers and feel at home in the spirit, even if you don't understand or speak the language! This is because you have the same Spirit, the Spirit of Christ. Ephesians 4:5-6 confirms this glorious truth. It states, "For the Lord God is one, and so are we, for we share in one faith, one baptism, and one Father. And he is the perfect Father who leads us all, works through us all, and lives in us all!". The Spirit of God is one, and in Christ we are one family, the family of God.

> *Having your identity in Christ means that any other identity you hyphenate after Christ is idolatry - ethnicity, race, profession, status, or political affiliation.*

CHAPTER 14
FALSE IDENTITY

False identity is often based on wrong self-definition. An individual can have an overriding affiliation that is so elevated or important to them in every circumstance, that it becomes highlighted and called out as their "identity". Some people allow their occupation, or position at work to elevate to such a level that it has an exaggerated role in their lives. They see their self-worth and value through the lens of their position. Others value themselves by their performance and are driven by what they are able to achieve. Others base their identity on financial wherewithal and the social status and power that come with it.

> *Our identity is not based on what we possess, rather, it is based on who possesses us.*

All these "identities" are flawed and tenuous at best, and these individuals are extremely vulnerable. Loss of or damage to any one of these "identities" can wreak untold havoc in that person's life. We all know real people or have watched movies of people who have committed untold atrocities in a flailing attempt to hold on to a vanishing image, position, social status, wealth or power. It is so pathetic and tragic to see, as their world unravels all around them, how they frantically clutch to the last vestiges of their "identity", desperately trying to hold onto the image of who they were. I heard Andrew Wommack tell the story of his early years in the ministry, when he would go to nursing homes to minister. He saw many different people, from different walks of life, all now living out their twilight years in the nursing home. He told of one particular woman, who was the wife of a well-known minister. She was always so well dressed and looked distinguished, but she was dejected and cried a lot. Andrew said that she would repeat, over and over again, "I used to be somebody". What a sad commentary about what happens when we live our lives with a faulty self-definition.

Below are some examples of wrong self-definition and faulty identities:

Possession: I AM because I have. This is an asset based identity. However, our true identity is not based on what we possess, rather, it is based on who possesses us. Jesus said that one's life does not consist in the abundance of the things which he possesses. So, our real identity is not in our possessions but in our heavenly Father.

Association: I AM the group I belong to or I AM because of the group I belong to. This is an association based identity, the wrong identity that drives young men to join gangs, or young women to get into or stay in unhealthy relationships that exploit them, just so they can "belong" or "be with" someone. This false identity is not only flawed and dysfunctional, it is dangerous!

Past: I AM my heritage or history. This is the false identity that defines a person by their past, history, sinful heritage, or generational curse running in their family. I recently counseled a beautiful and accomplished woman who tearfully told me, that as far back as she could remember, she does not have a family member who is married, with both parents at home. Her entire family lineage is made up of single moms, and now she is a divorced single mom, and struggling in her current relationship. I told her that she could be the first one in her family to have a healthy marriage, if she will say no to fear, reject selfishness, submit to God, work on her relationship and cancel those voices speaking from her past and ancestry. Her future does not have to echo her past, or the history of her natural family. She has a new family lineage, the lineage of Christ.

Limitation: I AM my inadequacy, failure, sins, or labels. I am the labels that society, school, culture or family members have placed on me. I am confined or constrained by a physical impairment or a perceived mental or emotional dysfunction. This wrong self-definition revolves around the word, "can't".

The children's book, "The Elephant and the Rope", tells the story of a man who passed by a circus and saw majestic elephants, tied to a stake by a thin rope. He was amazed that these huge creatures were being held by only a small rope tied to their front leg; no chains, cages, or walls. The elephants could, with a little tug, break free at any time; but for some reason, they didn't. He asked a trainer why these magnificent animals willingly stayed in captivity, and he explained that when they were very young and small, the same size rope was used to tie them, and at that age, it was enough to hold them. As they grew, they became conditioned to believe that they could not break away, so they never try to break free.

Imagine that! These animals could be free, but because they believed that they couldn't, they didn't even try. This is the power of a limitation, wrong belief system, or negative mindset. The mental conditioning they induce forge the bars of an invisible but extremely powerful prison that confines the individual. Labels like "failure", "always mess things up" or "never amount to anything", become a vice-like grip that can hold people captive for life, unless and until they decide to break free. Christ offers freedom from every bondage and limitation.

Opinion: I Am what people think or say of me. In today's social media world, human opinion is more pervasive than ever. People feel compelled to voice their opinion, even viciously, and those opinions have ruined countless lives. Human opinion is by far the most unstable and downright treacherous foundation to base your identity on! God's opinion is the only one that matters, and He loves, accepts, and approves of you.

Sickness: I AM my sickness, pain or dysfunction. This is the self-definition that is based on a malady. Often, whole communities of support and affinity develop around certain sicknesses and areas of dysfunction. While these communities play a great role in helping people successfully navigate the challenges of their present circumstances, if they are not careful, they can adopt these dysfunctions and the communities they foster as their identity. We see an example of this in John 5, when Jesus spoke to the lame man at the pool of Bethesda. This man's support group and community of care had become a crutch, and part of the story he tells himself to justify why he is the way he is. Over time, that story became a stronghold that kept him from getting well. I have heard people refer to different sicknesses in personal ownership terms, like "my" cancer, fibromyalgia, diabetes, and so on. The Bible says you shall have what you say. If you claim a sickness, then it is yours and you'll make room for it in your thinking and life.

Personally, I oppose sickness in all its forms. I declare that the blood of Jesus is on patrol 24/7 in my life and the lives of my children enforcing the covenant of life and health that we have in Christ. The blood is speaking abundant life to every cell, tissue and organ of our bodies. Death, disease, poverty, calamity and affliction cannot come into our lives and homes, they have to pass over because of the blood of Jesus. You see, I line up my words with the word of God and speak life over myself and my family. I challenge you to do the same.

Shame: I AM my mistake. These are the people who, goaded by the devil, define themselves by their worst mistake. They perennially carry the weight and painful feeling of humiliation, indignity and embarrassment of their prior blunder. Examples are people who define themselves as ex-convict, divorcee and addict. These tags become an invisible ceiling that the devil uses to clamp down on them and limit their potential. To break free, you must reject the "branding iron" of shame, and receive, believe, and appropriate God's love without reservations or caveats. Your identity is not in your past mistakes. Your identity is in Christ alone. Like Max Lucado said, "Haven't you shouldered that guilt long enough? Let grace happen for heaven's sake!"

> "Haven't you shouldered that guilt long enough? Let grace happen for heaven's sake!"

Circumstances: I AM my present circumstances. This is one of the most confining strategies of the devil, that leads to hopelessness despair and often, suicide. When people believe the lie that their present circumstances are permanent, that they are powerless to change it, and that there is no light at the end of the tunnel. Repeat disappointment can be devastating, beat a person down, and rob them of hope for a better future. They become emotionally exhausted and lose their will to fight. The truth is that with God all things are possible. He is able to bring beauty out of ashes. So, no matter how bad your situation looks, don't give up. When God is involved, things are never what they seem. He is the creator of the universe and your daddy. It's never over until He says so.

Loss of Identity

> *Reject the "branding iron" of shame, and receive, believe, and appropriate God's love without reservations or caveats.*

Sometimes, unforeseen events, changes in life circumstances or loss of a role that previously defined us, can cause an identity crisis. For example, getting divorced, becoming an empty nester, moving to a new city, losing a job, health issues, or experiencing a traumatic event can lead to a sense of self and identity loss. When we lose our identity and sense of self, it impacts our personal value, and we are likely to seek for self-worth from extrinsic sources like the approval of others, our performance, popularity, financial resources, looks, and so on.

One of my friends was a caretaker for his wife for a large part of their marriage. He took early retirement so he can care for her at home. When she passed, he lost his sense of purpose and personal value. He struggled with identity and self-definition. Who was he when he was no longer her caregiver? I see this a lot too with people who go through a divorce. Many flounder as they struggle to determine who they are now, if they are not a wife or husband. For many, the role of husband or wife was so fundamental to their self-definition that they are disoriented for a long time after their divorce.

This is why it is so important to have our identity rooted and grounded in the unchanging person, love and word of God. When we draw our identity and sense of self from our relationship with Christ, it is a sure and unshakable foundation. Then, we have a solid sense of self which flows from God, and does not depend on our works, looks, status, performance, or people's expectations. People vacillate, but God does not. He is constant, and His affirmation and approval are unwavering.

Having a solid sense of self means being able to receive information about other people's opinions about us and being able to separate that from what we think and believe about ourselves. It also includes being able to maintain our individual identity, separate and distinct from the many roles or "hats" we wear in life. Some signs of identity loss include, losing passion for things you valued previously, constantly seeking the approval of others, negative self-talk, lack of self-care or "me" time, and becoming a chameleon to blend in with others or to become what they want you to be.

> *Our identity must be rooted and grounded in the unchanging person, love and word of God.*

People can also lose their identity through the devil's identity theft. In my book, "*Choosing a Life of Victory*", I outline in detail, the devil's multi-step identity theft strategy.

> *We can DO, because we ARE!*

Who Vs Do

One thing that can lead to false identity or loss of identity is when people confuse their WHO with their DO. We live in a culture where there is a hyper focus on doing. If you announce to your family, friends and co-workers that you are going on vacation, you are immediately bombarded with a barrage of questions about what you are going to DO. It's like you can't just BE on vacation. You must be doing something.

It seems that for many people, they are "human doings" and not "human beings". It's these same people who answer the question, "Who are you?" not with their "being", but with their "doing". They say things like, I am a nurse, mom, dad, wife, and so on. This type of confusion can lead to a loss of identity when they are no longer able to perform the role or occupation that had defined them. God on the other hand is focused on our being. He is not impressed by our ability, performance, or accomplishments. He values us because of who we are, and not what we do, have or who we know; but simply because we are His sons and daughters!

Ephesians 2:8-10 says is succinctly! God saved us by his grace when we believed. And we can't take credit for this; it is a gift from God. Salvation is not a reward for the good things we have done, so none of us can boast about it. For **we are** God's masterpiece. He has created us anew in Christ Jesus, so **we can do** the good things he planned for us long ago. We can do, because we are!

The Wild, Wild, West

I like the old western movies. They are set in simpler times, when wholesome family values were the norm. So, they are for the most part clean and the incidents of violence are relatively mild. A common story line in many of the series is a loss of identity. A cowboy would be thrown from his horse and hit his head, or suffer some other trauma that leads to amnesia, dislocation of his sense of self, and a loss of identity. Because people act consistent with who they believe they are, anyone who doesn't know who they are can do almost anything. They typically suffer from the following:

1. Severe disorientation, confusion and anxiety. They don't know how to act.

2. They take on or adopt the character and lifestyle of whoever they are with. Since they don't know who they are, they have no frame of reference to guide their choices and no sense of self or value system to direct or constrain them.

3. They are easily deceived, used, and abused. They are vulnerable and very gullible. People often take advantage of them, and lie to them about who they are; and because they don't know better, they believe them and act accordingly.

4. People who don't know who they are can do anything. In one episode, a renowned attorney from a wealthy family became

a lowly cow hand, because he didn't know who he was. In the movie "Jericho", an upstanding sheriff with a loving family, became a fugitive on the run, living outside the law and drifting from place to place for 7 years, because he had been hit in the head, lost his memory and was led to believe that he was a robber and murderer.

5. People who do not know who they are feel that they don't belong anywhere.

6. Often, they can't plan for the future because they don't know their past, dreams or aspirations, and they have problems making decisions because they have gaps in their decision making framework. They don't know their likes, dislikes, values, strengths and weaknesses.

This is why identity and self-knowledge are so important, and this is why the devil works so hard to make people believe lies about themselves, because the lies you believe become your reality. Sadly, he has used this strategy of lies and deception to limit so many Christians and rob them of their identity and inheritance in God.

> *People act consistent with who they believe they are, so anyone who doesn't know who they are can do almost anything.*

CHAPTER 15
REJECTION

Rejection is in epidemic proportions in today's world. It is a word that refers to feelings of shame, sadness, alienation, or grief that a person suffers when they are not accepted by others. It also includes the negative feeling a person experiences when disappointed about not achieving something desired. Rejection can occur in the context of a romantic interest, or in social, group or family settings, or in the professional world in relation to advancement. It inflicts emotional pain and can lead to anger, anxiety, depression, jealousy, sadness, poor self-image, and low self-esteem. It can breed uncertainty and fear - fear of further or future rejection. People who have repeatedly been rejected can develop a sensitivity to rejection such that they misinterpret, distort and overreact to what other people say and do. At its core, rejection is an attack against identity.

> Rejection is an attack against identity.

Nobody likes rejection, but it is a fact of life. In today's society, there is hyper sensitivity to criticism and rejection. Social media has significantly heightened this phenomenon and can trigger devastating consequences. Rejection can and has been weaponized by online mobs to destroy the lives of people. It's called cancel culture. This is a modern form of ostracism in which someone is rejected and thrust out of social or professional circles -

either online on social media, in the real world, or both. Canceled people have lost their livelihoods and some have had to uproot themselves and their families.

Take Justine Sacco, a public relations executive who tweeted, "Going to Africa. Hope I don't get AIDS. Just kidding. I'm white!" while waiting at the London airport to board her flight to South Africa. No one replied to that tweet and so Justine got on her plane and turned off her phone. She turned it back on when she landed in Cape Town, only to realize that her life was ruined. Someone from her 174 followers sent the tweet to someone else and started a chain reaction. Justine was vilified by thousands of people raging at her on twitter. Then her boss called to say she was fired, and her mom said some ugly things to her. What about Adam Mark Smith, who was rude to a Chick-Fil-A worker on YouTube? Well, he had to sell his house and move to a new city.

Heightened fear of rejection is an emotional health issue. It is called Rejection Sensitive Dysphoria or RSD. This is extreme emotional sensitivity and pain triggered by the perception that a person has been rejected or criticized by important people in their life. It may also be triggered by a sense of falling short, failing to meet their own high standards or other people's expectations. Symptoms include; low self-esteem; avoidance of social settings; fear of failure; overly high expectations for self; frequent emotional outbursts; feelings of hopelessness, approval-seeking behavior; aggression in uncomfortable situations and anxiety.

Free from People

The root of rejection is seeking the approval, support, or affirmation of people, or basing your identity or self-definition on how other people see, perceive or appraise you. This is called social identity. When we elevate the opinion or acceptance of people in our lives, then their rejection can be devastating. Knowing your identity in Christ and being secure in your heavenly Father's affirmation can shield you from the deleterious impact of human rejection. Jesus said, those the Father has given me will come to me, and I will never reject them. All who come to me, I will embrace and will never turn them away (John 6:37). Jesus will never reject you.

So, we must look to Him and not people for approval. We must draw our sense of self, acceptance, and personal validation from our heavenly Father, and not from people in our lives or "friends" on social media. This is important because if people's approval cannot define, validate or confirm me, then neither can their disapproval, rejection or ridicule invalidate or genuinely diminish me, unless I let it. It has only the weight I ascribe to it, and I can elect to deprive it of any weight and power to hurt or negatively impact me. Even if the individual's express goal and intent was to diminish or neutralize me, I can refuse to be diminished, and in so doing completely rob their actions of power (*Single and Happy*).

Jesus did not look to people for approval. In John 5:41, He said, "I do not receive honor from men." He did not try to convince people of His value or look to them to validate Him. He knew who he was! In John 2:23–25, the Bible states: "Now while he was in Jerusalem at the Passover Festival, many people saw the signs He was performing and believed in His name. But Jesus would not entrust Himself to them, for He knew all people. He did not need any testimony about mankind, for He knew what was in each person." Jesus was free from people! Knowledge of who He was freed Him from human opinions, good or bad, and released Him to fulfill His mission.

> *If people's approval cannot define, validate or confirm me, then neither can their disapproval, rejection or ridicule invalidate or genuinely diminish me, unless I let it.*

Stoned God

In Acts 14:8-20, we see a sad illustration of the danger of basing your identity on the view or approval of people. At Lystra, apostle Paul and Barnabas healed a crippled man. This man had been crippled from birth. As he listened to Paul preach, "Paul realized he had faith to be healed. So, Paul called to him in a loud voice, "Stand up!" And the man jumped to his feet and started walking." When the crowd saw this miraculous healing, they shouted in their local dialect, "These men are gods in human form!" They decided that Barnabas was the Greek god Zeus and that Paul was Hermes, since he was the chief speaker. The priest of Zeus and the crowd brought bulls and wreaths to offer sacrifices to the apostles.

Paul and Barnabas were distraught at this brazen display of idolatry and raced to stop them. They were barely able to restrain the people from making sacrifices to them. Soon after, some Jews arrived from Antioch and Iconium and won the crowds over to their side. They stoned Paul and dragged him out of town, thinking he was dead. Imagine that! The same crowd that called him a god and wanted to sacrifice to him, now stoned him and left him for dead! That is the danger of putting any stock in human approval.

People's approval is as fleeting as the vapor of smoke. Jesus knew this all too well. The same crowd that hailed Him and shouted "Hosanna" on Palm Sunday when He rode into Jerusalem on a donkey, shouted "crucify him" the very next week. We must put our trust and confidence in God and not man.

So, do not base your self-esteem on people's opinions. Believe what God says about you, and never let insecurity or the fear of rejection run your life. You are good enough, smart enough, beautiful enough, and strong enough. You are enough! Become so confident in who you are in Christ that no one's opinions, rejection, or behavior can rock or destabilize you. Make friends with yourself and the God who lives inside you, and you will never be truly rejected or alone ever!

In Christ, you are enough!

Knowing Who You Are Not

A key piece of answering the question "Who are you" is knowing who you are not. That knowledge clarifies your identity perception and is a major protection against rejection. For John the Baptist, knowing who he was, and who he was not, protected him from rejection, temptation, and sin. John 1:19-22 states that:

The Jewish leaders sent an entourage of priests and temple servants from Jerusalem to interrogate John. They asked him, "Who are you?" John answered them directly, saying, "I am not the Messiah!" "Then who are you?" they asked. "Are you Elijah?" "No," John replied. So they pressed him further, "Are you the prophet Moses said was coming, the one we're expecting?" "No," he replied. "Then who are you?" they demanded. John responded in the words of the prophet Isaiah, "I am the voice in the wilderness saying prepare the way of the Lord."

John knew who he was, and who he was not. That knowledge protected him from competition, distraction, and going off on a tangent. Knowing who you are grounds you and gives you a sense of purpose and mission. It also protects your time, resources and emotional energy reserves from being depleted, and conserves them for the important work God has given to you. It gives you focus and alignment. When you know who you are, you do not need people to tell you who you are. And when you know who you are not, you can quickly discern what does or does not align with your set purpose.

> *Sometimes, what is mis-diagnosed as rejection is God's redirection.*

John's clarity about his identity protected him from competing with Jesus. In John 3:25-30, the Bible records that John's disciples came to him and said, "Rabbi, the man you met on the other side of the Jordan River, the one you identified as the Messiah, is also baptizing people. And everybody is going to him instead of coming to us." They expected John to be up in arms and get into a turf war with Jesus. After all, John was there first. But John knew who he was, and who he was not. He calmly replied, "You yourselves know how I plainly told you, 'I am not the Messiah. I am only here to prepare the way for him.' Therefore, I am filled with joy at his success. He must become greater and greater, and I must become less and less." Wow!

Knowing who he was protected him from jealousy, envy, contention and competition. In fact, when he pointed Jesus out as the Lamb of God, two of his disciples left him and followed Jesus. John did not run after them or accuse Jesus of stealing his flock. He stayed true to his calling and secure in his identity.

Jesus also modeled this resolute self-knowledge and identity security. Knowing who He was protected Him from the devil's temptations and from trying to perform for human acclaim. Knowledge of His identity and purpose also enabled Jesus to look at Peter, His foremost disciple, and say to him, "get behind me Satan" when he tried to keep Jesus from going to the cross; and to call Judas, the man who betrayed Him, "friend" when he came with the chief priests to arrest Him (Matthew 16:23; 26:48-50). Jesus knew who He was, and realized that Peter's "protection", though well-meaning, was completely contrary to his set purpose and divine assignment, and Judas' betrayal, though engineered by the devil, was actually furthering His mission, and the plan and purpose of God for the redemption of mankind.

> *When God gives you a new beginning, it starts with an ending.*

Rejection Mis-Diagnoses

Rejection is sometimes mis-diagnosed. Often what you think is rejection directed towards you by another person, is really a manifestation of that person's insecurity. Many people are insecure and unsure of themselves. So, in social settings, they appear aloof, detached, snobbish and even hostile. Others interpret that as rejection and a lack of desire to associate with and accept them. But the truth is, it's really not about you. They have problems of their own that range from lack of self-acceptance, to feelings of inferiority, and low self-esteem. So, when people appear to reject you, most of the time, they are really intimidated by you; and what looks to you like rejection, is their attempt to protect themselves from making a fool of themselves in what they perceive to be your superior presence. On the surface, it appeared that King Saul hated and rejected David and tried to kill him; but the truth is that he was grossly insecure and deathly afraid of David's potential and the favor of God on his life.

Sometimes, what is mis-diagnosed as rejection is God's redirection. Closed doors are one of God's means of redirecting us to something or someone better. If you are looking for a relationship, job, or opportunity, and are turned down or lose out to someone else, don't be devastated. God is working behind the scenes. He is the one who opens doors for friendship, relationship, kingdom connections, and new opportunities. Revelation 3:7 says that He has "the key of David" and what He opens, no one can close; and what He closes, no one can open. God will open the right doors for you at the right time. He can also close doors that He doesn't want you to go through. When He closes a door, thank Him and praise Him in the hallway. If you insist on kicking down a door that God has closed, you are on your own, and will bring needless pain into your life. Trust that when God closes a door, whatever is behind it is not for your good.

Sometimes, God closes a door because it's time to move forward. He knows you won't move unless your circumstances force you to. Someone has said that when God gives you a new beginning, it starts with an ending. If you want the new, you have to be willing to let go of the old. So, make room and stay alert for whatever God will do next. Always remain suspicious that God is up to something good. That is expectancy, trust and hope; and this hope will not disappoint because our God is the Way-Maker, Miracle Worker, Promise Keeper, and Light in the darkness. So, be thankful for closed doors. They often guide us to the right one!

Knowing your identity frees you from anxiety over closed doors, rejection, jealousy, envy, contention and competition, and helps you to keep your eyes on God and trust Him with your future.

> *Knowing who you are grounds you and gives you a sense of purpose, mission, focus and alignment.*

THE MISSING LINK – PROCLAMATIONS
SAYING THE SAME THING ABOUT YOURSELF AS GOD
30 DAY PROCLAMATION OF YOUR IDENTITY IN CHRIST

I AM A CHILD OF GOD

Scripture

For all who are led by the Spirit of God are children of God. So, you have not received a spirit that makes you fearful slaves. Instead, you received God's Spirit when he adopted you as his own children. Now we call him, "Abba, Father." For his Spirit joins with our spirit to affirm that we are God's children - Romans 8:14-17.

Proclamation

I AM a child of God! I am an offspring of God. In Him, I live and move and have my being. I am born again, by the incorruptible seed of the word of God. I am born into greatness. I am an heir of God and a joint heir with Christ. I have the DNA of Almighty God. I am a partaker of His divine nature. My identity is not in my possessions, performance, position, status, looks, or popularity. My identity is in Christ and Christ alone. I refuse to answer to any labels, limits or stereotypes that any man or woman may want to place on me. I break out of every box of human definition and limitation. I look the devil, sin, the world, and the flesh in the eye and declare, I BELONG TO GOD, and I answer to only one label, title and name – child of the Most-High God!

_____

_____

_____

_____

I AM COMPLETE IN CHRIST

Scripture

For in Christ lives all the fullness of God in a human body. So you also are complete through your union with Christ, who is the head over every ruler and authority – Colossians 2:10.

Proclamation

I AM complete in Christ! I am seated in heavenly places in Christ Jesus, far above every rule, authority, power, or dominion, not only in this world, but in the world to come. In Christ lives all the fullness of God in human form. He is the embodiment of all the attributes of God, and I am completely filled with God as Christ's fullness overflows within me. I am a God-carrying vessel, filled with the maximum load of God! I do not look outside of myself and Christ who lives in me, for my sense of self-worth, validation, confidence, affirmation, and wellbeing. I am self-sufficient in Christ's sufficiency. I do not look to anyone or anything else to complete me or make me happy. I am complete in Christ. In Him, I AM ENOUGH!

_____

_____

_____

_____

_____

I AM THE RIGHTEOUSNESS OF GOD

Scripture

For He made Jesus who knew no sin *to be* sin for us, that we might become the righteousness of God in Him - 2 Corinthians 5:21.

Proclamation

I AM the righteousness of God in Christ! God made Jesus, the only one who never sinned, to become sin for me, so that I might become the righteousness of God through my union with Him. I receive and appropriate the righteousness of Christ. Sin is no longer my master! I put off my old sinful nature and my former way of life, and I put on my new nature, created to be like God, truly righteous and holy. I am righteous, and live righteously, according to my new nature, the nature of God in me. I reject and renounce all bitterness, lying, stealing, rage, anger, harsh words, and slander, as well as all types of evil behavior. Instead, I will be kind, tenderhearted, forgiving others, just as God through Christ has forgiven me. I AM the righteousness of God. I will not use foul or abusive language. I will not bring sorrow to God's Holy Spirit by the way I live.

I AM A NEW CREATION IN CHRIST

Scripture

Therefore, if anyone *is* in Christ, *he is* a new creation; old things have passed away; behold, all things have become new - 2 Corinthians 5:18.

Proclamation

I AM a new creation in Christ! Jesus Christ is my Lord and Savior. I am redeemed, not with mere silver or gold, which lose their value, but with the precious blood of Christ, the sinless, spotless, Lamb of God. In my spirit, I look exactly like Jesus because I am joined with Him. I celebrate my spiritual life and identity in Christ. I have God's Spirit, the Holy Spirit, living in me. I have a new heart, a heart that loves and treasures the word of God. I have spiritual ears, that hear what the Holy Spirit is saying. I have new eyes that see in the spirit. I have a new mind, the mind of Christ. In Jesus's name, I reject old patterns of thought, mindsets, strongholds, habits and sinful desires, and declare that I walk in newness of life. I take authority over every voice speaking against me from my past and human ancestry, and drown them with the voice of the blood of Jesus. I shut down every accusation from the devil. I walk in the light, as God is in the light; I have fellowship with Him, and Jesus' blood cleanses me of all sin.

I AM LOVED BY GOD

Scripture

I have loved you, with an everlasting love. With unfailing love I have drawn you to myself - Jeremiah 31:3.

Proclamation

I AM loved by God with a lavish, extravagant, and everlasting love! God demonstrated His great love toward me, in that while I was still a sinner, Christ died for me. How deeply intimate and far-reaching is His love! How enduring and inclusive it is! Endless love beyond measurement that transcends my understanding. Unconditional love that knows no limitations, reservations, or obstacles. This love pours into me until I am filled to overflowing with the fullness of God! Today, I believe and receive the love of God; and declare that my roots grow down deep into His love and keep me strong. I have the power to understand how wide, how long, how high, and how deep His love is, and I am made complete with all the fullness of life and power that comes from God.

_____

_____

_____

_____

_____

_____

I AM ROYALTY

Scripture

But you are a chosen people, a royal priesthood, a holy nation, God's special possession, that you may declare the praises of him who called you out of darkness into his wonderful light -1 Peter 2:9.

Proclamation

I AM hand-picked, selected and chosen by Almighty God; I am His special treasure, I am royalty! God has made me a priest and a king in His kingdom. He called me out of darkness to experience His marvelous light, and He identified, announced and publicly acknowledged me as His very own. I belong to God and my identity flow from Him! My Father is the King of kings and Lord of Lords. The whole earth belongs to Him, and everything in it. He is the sovereign ruler of the universe. He has called me to showcase His glorious love, grace, power, and wonders throughout the world. I AM royalty! I, who at one time did not know God, has now become God's delight, a child of the King, a joyful recipient of God's grace, and drenched with His love and mercy. Once I had no identity as a person; now I am identified as a child of God. Hallelujah!

_____

_____

_____

_____

_____

I AM PRECIOUS TO GOD

Scripture

Since you are precious and honored in my sight, and because I love you, I will give people in exchange for you, nations in exchange for your life - Isaiah 43:4.

Proclamation

I AM precious to God! God gave Jesus, the very best that heaven has for me. He believes in me, and empowers me to believe in myself. I am a person greatly beloved. Jesus gave His life for me, that is the measure of my worth and value. God is on my side. God is for me, He is not against me. No good thing will He withhold from me. God has blessed me and wants to be good to me. I am His beloved child in whom He is well pleased. God has released his omnipotent power and deployed His angels to watch over me and war on my behalf. He is with me, and will move heaven and earth to help me. I am more than a conqueror through Christ. God has made me prosperous in wealth and in health. I walk in abundance and overflow. I can do all things through Christ. God's plan is to give me and my family a good life and a great future.

_____

_____

_____

_____

_____

I AM KNOWN

Scripture

Before I formed you in the womb, I knew you, and before you were born, I consecrated you - Jeremiah 1:5.

Proclamation

I AM deeply and intimately known by God! Lord, you examine my heart and know everything about me. You know when I sit down or stand up. You know my thoughts. You know everything I do. You know what I am going to say before I say it. You place your hand of blessing on my head. You are not embarrassed or disappointed by me. You know my failures, public and private, you know the things that make me cry, you know the things I am ashamed of, but you never reject me or diminish your attention toward me. You tenderly stroke my hair and count the hairs on my head. When I cry, you scrape every tear and save it in your bottle. You think about me all the time. Your thoughts about me are countless, like the sands on the seashore. There is no place so dark, so deep, so high or so far that you are not there. No place I can go, that you won't go with me. I do not want to be anywhere, do anything, or be with anyone that will distract me from your presence.

_____

_____

_____

_____

I AM OF TREMENDOUS WORTH AND VALUE

Scripture

For you know that God paid a ransom to save you from the empty life you inherited from your ancestors. And it was not paid with mere gold or silver, which lose their value. It was the precious blood of Christ, the sinless, spotless Lamb of God – 1 Peter 1:18-19.

Proclamation

I HAVE tremendous worth and value! I am a child of Almighty God! My value comes from my source. It does not come from my performance, whether or not people like me, how much money I have, who I know, what I drive, how I look, or where I live. God is my source of origin, and that source will never diminish in value. I don't need to convince people of my value. Jesus already did that. I simply own my value. I will not discount myself or sell myself short. I will not waste my time with, or give myself to people who do not value me. God made me an original, I will not be a cheap copy. I am an uncommon package, with my temperament, personality, quirks, skin color, and ethnicity. I was uniquely put together by God. Nothing about me is an accident. I am one of a kind. Nothing and no one can truly devalue me, because my value comes from God. Jesus paid full price for me. I will not give myself away at a discount!

_____

_____

_____

_____

I AM FREE FROM PEOPLE

Scripture

Jesus said, your approval means nothing to me. I do not accept the honor that comes from men - John 5:41.

Proclamation

I AM free from people, like Jesus was free from people! I do not look to people for approval, validation, acceptance or applause. I do not lean, rely on or draw my self-image or self- esteem from human opinion, good or bad. The approval of people cannot define, validate or confirm me, and their disapproval, rejection or ridicule cannot invalidate or genuinely diminish me. They are not God, so, their opinion doesn't matter and their approval is not needed! I renounce every need or craving for human approval. I have Almighty God's approval and His approval does not depend on my works, looks, performance, or people's expectations. People are fickle, but God is not. He is constant, and His approval is unwavering. In Jesus name, I inaugurate a fast from the praise, approval, or validation of people. I declare, that I AM free from the definitions, labels, stereotypes, opinions, affirmations or rejection of people, and the world!

_____

_____

_____

_____

I AM THE GOD KIND

Scripture

Then God said, let us make human beings in our image, to be like us... So, God created human beings in his own image. In the image of God he created them; male and female he created them – Genesis1:26-28.

Proclamation

I AM the Godkind! God reproduced me after His own kind. He made me only a little lower than Himself and crowned me with glory and honor. He put me in charge over everything He made, and put all things under my authority. I have His attributes and nature, and can manifest His power. I am His offspring! It is through him that I live and function and have my identity; my lineage comes from him. I look exactly like Jesus in my spirit. As He is, so am I in this world. I am the image of God. I know my identity in Christ and I walk in it. God has commissioned me to occupy and rule over the earth, acting in His stead. I will faithfully execute that assignment. I AM the god-kind. I say NO to sin, the world, my flesh and the devil. I say NO to sickness, poverty, calamity, bondage or limitation. I say YES to God's plan, presence, purpose, passion and power.

_____

_____

_____

_____

I AM KEPT BY GOD

Scripture

You are kept by the power of God through faith for salvation ready to be revealed in the last time - 1 Peter 1:5.

Proclamation

I AM kept by the power of God! I am upheld by the omnipotent hand of God. Thank you, Lord, for all the things I went through, that could have destroyed me; all the times I was down to nothing; all the times I wanted to give up, but was empowered to take another step; and all the times, when the devil had me in a corner and was coming in for the kill, BUT GOD intervened, just in the nick of time. I am kept by the power of God. The Lord is my keeper. As the mountains surround Jerusalem, so the Lord surrounds me. God has given His angels orders to keep me in all my ways. He will not allow my foot to slip or to be moved; He Who keeps me does not slumber. Yes, He who keeps me and my family will not slumber nor sleep. The Lord is my keeper; He is my shade on my right hand. The sun shall not smite me by day, nor the moon by night. The Lord will keep me from all evil; He will keep my life. The Lord will keep my going out and my coming in from this time forth and forevermore.

_____

_____

_____

_____

I AM PROTECTED

Scripture

The name of the LORD *is* a strong tower; the righteous run to it and are safe – Proverbs 18:10.

Proclamation

I AM protected! I dwell in the secret place of the Most High, I abide under the shadow of the Almighty. I declare that the LORD alone is my refuge, my place of safety; my God, and I trust Him. He rescues me from every trap and protects me from deadly disease. He covers me with His feathers, He shelters me with His wings. His faithful promises are my armor and protection. I am not afraid of the terrors of the night, nor the arrows that fly in the day. I do not dread the disease that stalks in darkness, nor the disaster that strikes at midday. Though a thousand fall at my side, and ten thousand are dying around me, these evils will not touch me. I just open my eyes, and see how the wicked are punished. Because I have made the LORD my refuge, and the Most High my shelter, no evil will conquer me; no plague will come near my home. God has ordered His angels to protect me and minister to me wherever I go. The LORD rescues and protects me who trust in His name.

_____

_____

_____

_____

I AM APPROVED

Scripture

Everyone who believes has God's approval through Faith in Jesus Christ – Romans 3:22.

Proclamation

I AM accepted and approved! Almighty God has approved of me! He approved of me before anybody else had a chance to disapprove, and His approval is unconditional and unwavering. I recognize that not everyone will understand, support or approve of me, and that is okay. I have God's approval! My heavenly Father has selected, affirmed and confirmed his love, blessing and favor on me. It doesn't matter who does not accept or approve of me. God is for me, who can be against me? The Creator of heaven and earth has determined to stand with me, tell me, who could ever stand against me? God's approval empowers me! God's favor will take me to new heights, open new doors for me, position me for increase, elevate me, announce me and move me to new levels of influence! In Christ, I AM enough! I am good enough, smart enough, strong enough, and attractive enough. In Christ, I AM Enough!

I AM A WINNER

Scripture

The LORD will make you the head and not the tail, and you will always be on top and never at the bottom – Deuteronomy 28:13.

Proclamation

I AM a winner! I have strength for all things in Christ. I am ready for anything and equal to anything through Christ who infuses inner strength into me; I am self-sufficient in Christ's sufficiency. I am anointed to prosper and empowered to succeed. I have the spirit of excellence, a winner's attitude and great work ethic! I am motivated, confident, and driven to manifest all the excellencies of God. I call forth into my life all the human, material, financial and relational resources that I need to fully accomplish God's plan and purpose for my life. I am physically, mentally, and emotionally ready for the new things God has planned for me. My steps are ordered and directed by the Lord. I am starting over, with a new thought pattern, positive emotions, strong connection to the Lord, and a new faith and confidence in myself. God will not allow anyone to derail me or keep me from destiny. In every challenge and situation, overwhelming victory is mine through Christ, who loves me.

_____

_____

_____

_____

I AM HIS SHEEP AND HEAR HIS VOICE

Scripture

My sheep listen to my voice; I know them, and they follow me – John 10:27.

Proclamation

I AM His sheep and I hear His voice! Lord Jesus, I hear your voice and follow you joyfully. I have a discerning ear. I hear your voice through your word, through prayer, and the Holy Spirit who lives in me. I am willing and obedient to your instructions. I am a doer of the word and not a hearer only. My life is in alignment with Your plan and purpose. I AM your sheep and I do recognize your voice. I will never be lost and no one can snatch me out of your hands. A stranger's voice I will not hear. I will not listen to seducing spirits or doctrines of devils. I will not listen to the voice of the accuser, shame, anxiety, fear, and reproach. I will not listen to the voice of the world system, or my sinful desires. Rather, I hear the voice of God saying, "this is the way, walk in it". Thank you, Lord, that you have given me the tongue of a disciple; that I should know how to speak the right words, at the right time, to the right people. You wake me up, every morning, and cause me to hear as a disciple.

_____

_____
_____

_____

I AM FREE FROM GUILT AND CONDEMNATION

Scripture

There is therefore now no condemnation to those who are in Christ Jesus, who do not walk according to the flesh, but according to the Spirit - Romans 8:1.

Proclamation

I AM free from guilt and condemnation! God has justified me! To Him, it is just as if I had never sinned. There is no condemnation for me because I belong to Christ. I proclaim Tetelestai! My sin debt is PAID IN FULL!!! Jesus paid for my every sin, infraction, iniquity and transgression, and has set me free. I reject the lies and accusations of the devil. I am the elect of God, holy and beloved! Who can bring any charge against me, since God Himself has justified me? God has given me right standing with Himself, who then will condemn me? My conscience is clean and clear, and I walk in the glorious liberty of the children of God. I AM free and empowered to make better, healthier and more biblical choices and decisions. I take my joy, peace, happiness, and freedom back. Every voice that rises up against me in judgement, I condemn!

_____

_____

_____

_____

I AM REDEEMED FROM EVERY CURSE

Scripture

But Christ has rescued us from the curse pronounced by the law. When he was hung on the cross, he took upon himself the curse for our wrongdoing. For it is written in the Scriptures, "Cursed is everyone who is hung on a tree – Galatians 3:13.

Proclamation

I AM free from every curse! Jesus has delivered me from the curse pronounced by the law. When He hung on the cross, He took upon Himself the curse for my wrongdoing. He canceled the record of all charges against me and nailed it to His cross. He disarmed powers, principalities, the spiritual rulers and authorities and shamed them publicly by His victory over them on the cross. I reject, renounce, cancel, terminate, and overthrow every curse, hex, omen, spell, generational curse, or satanic covenant operating in my life and family. I bind, demolish and obliterate every witchcraft, divination, incantation or magic spells against me and my family. I shut down the operation of every wicked spirit supervising and enforcing any curse, dysfunction or bondage in my life and family. Jesus has set me free, and I am free indeed. I am blessed, I cannot be cursed. My blessing is irreversible. I have the blessings of Abraham.

I AM BLESSED

Scripture

All praise to God, the Father of our Lord Jesus Christ, who has blessed us with every spiritual blessing in the heavenly realms because we are united with Christ - Ephesians 1:3.

Proclamation

I AM blessed, prosperous, strong, favored, successful, productive, vigorous, fruitful, and wealthy! All the blessings of God pursue and overtake me. I am blessed in the city and blessed in the suburbs, blessed going out and blessed coming in. I am blessed in my mind, will and emotions. I walk in abundance, increase and overflow. I am blessed physically, spiritually, financially, socially, intellectually, relationally, and influentially. My cup overflows! My children and family are blessed. Wherever we go and whatever we do, we are supernaturally blessed. The LORD has commanded a guaranteed blessing on my life. I stand under open heavens. I will lend to many, but will not need to borrow. The LORD has made me the head and not the tail, always on top and never at the bottom. I am empowered to succeed and anointed to prosper. God's covenant of blessing, favor, grace and peace will never be broken in my life.

I AM FEARLESS

Scripture

For God has not given us a spirit of fear and timidity, but of power, love, and self-discipline – 2 Timothy 1:7.

Proclamation

I AM fearless! God has not given me a spirit of fear, but of power, love, and sound mind. I say NO to fear in all its forms. I reject every spirit of bondage to fear. God is my refuge and strength, my very present help in trouble, so, I will not fear. The LORD is my light and my salvation, so whom shall I fear? The Lord is my fortress, protecting me from danger, so why should I fear or tremble? The LORD is for me, I will not fear, what can mere people do to me? God Himself has said, that He will not in any way fail me, nor give me up, nor leave me without support. He will never leave me helpless, or forsake me, or let me down, or relax His hold on me! So, I take comfort and I am encouraged and I confidently and boldly say, the Lord is my Helper; I will not panic, fear, worry or be terrified. What can man do to me? Hallelujah! I have no fear, for the Lord is with me. I am not discouraged, for the Lord is my God. He strengthens, helps and upholds me with His victorious right hand.

_____

_____

_____

_____

I AM COURAGEOUS

Scripture

This is my command, be strong and courageous! Do not be afraid or discouraged. For the LORD your God is with you wherever you go - Joshua 1:9.

Proclamation

I AM bold and courageous! The Lord, my God is with me. Because He is at my right hand, I shall not be moved. I am not discouraged. I am steadfast, firm, and immovable. My heart is fixed, trusting in the Lord. The Lord Himself goes before me and is with me, I am never alone. I am on my guard; I stand firm in faith; I am courageous, and I am strong! In God I have put my trust and confidently take refuge; I shall never be put to shame or confusion! The Lord has strengthened my hands for war and my fingers to fight. I take a stand for righteousness, and speak up in the name of the Lord. I am a bold witness for Christ, and a courageous soldier of the cross. I do not cast away my confidence in God, which has a great reward. I know that the battle is not mine, the battle is the Lord's. He will fight for me, and I will hold my peace. With God's help I will fight like a hero, for He has trampled down my enemies.

I AM STRONG

Scripture

Be strong in the Lord and in his mighty power – Ephesians 6:10.

Proclamation

I AM strong in the Lord and in His mighty power! God has unleashed within me the unlimited riches of His glory and favor. His supernatural strength floods my innermost being with His divine might and explosive power! The Lord is on my side, He is among those who help me, therefore I know that I will triumph over all my enemies. It is better to trust and take refuge in the Lord than to put confidence in man. It is better to trust and take refuge in the Lord than to put confidence in princes. My enemies surrounded me to attack me, but in the name of the Lord I have cut them off! They surrounded me on every side; but in the name of the Lord I have cut them off! You, my adversary, thrust sorely at me that I might fall, but the Lord helped me. The Lord is my Strength and Song; and He has become my Salvation. Shouts of rejoicing are in my home. The Lord has done for me great things. The right hand of the Lord does valiantly and achieves strength! The right hand of the Lord is exalted. I shall not die but live, and declare the works of the Lord.

_____

_____

_____

_____

I AM A WARRIOR

Scripture

We are human, but we don't wage war as humans do. We use God's mighty weapons, not worldly weapons, to knock down the strongholds of human reasoning and to destroy false arguments – 2 Corinthians 10:3-4.

Proclamation

I AM a warrior for Christ! I am a soldier of the cross. I am not fighting against flesh-and-blood enemies, but against evil rulers, authorities, cosmic powers of darkness, and spiritual forces in the heavens. I stand strong and victorious with the force of Christ's explosive power flowing in and through me. I put on God's complete set of armor, so I am protected as I fight against the evil strategies of the devil! I put on truth as a belt to strengthen me, and righteousness as the protective armor that covers my heart. I stand on my feet alert, always ready to share the gospel of peace. In every battle, I take faith as my wrap-around shield, to extinguish the blazing arrows of the evil one! I put on the knowledge of who I am in Christ as a helmet to protect my thoughts from Satan's lies. I take the mighty, razor-sharp, sword of the Spirit, the spoken Word of God, and pray passionately in the Spirit. Thanks be to God for the victory in Christ!

_____
_____
_____
_____

I AM POWERFUL

Scripture

For the kingdom of God is not just a lot of talk, it is living by God's power - 1 Corinthians 4:20.

Proclamation

I AM Powerful! I have supernatural power. God's mighty power is at work in me to accomplish great things. Living in me is Christ who floods me with his glorious, inexhaustible power! I am a body wholly filled and flooded with God Himself! Embedded within me, is a heavenly treasure chest filled with the riches of God's glory, power, might, authority, dominion and excellence. God's miraculous power constantly energizes me. The same mighty power that raised Jesus from the dead, lives inside of me. This limitless, unstoppable power of Almighty God is working mightily in me. Jesus has given me power and authority over all the power of the devil. I take the limits off! I choose to believe for great things. Eyes have not seen, ears have not heard, and no mind has imagined what God has prepared for me. I believe, receive and appropriate them today. God's power in me, will achieve infinitely more than my greatest request, my most unbelievable dream, and exceed my wildest imagination!

I AM FREE FROM BONDAGE

Scripture

So Christ has truly set us free. Now make sure that you stay free, and don't get tied up again with a yoke of bondage – Galatians 5:1.

Proclamation

I AM free from bondage! Jesus Christ has set me free, and I am free indeed. I take authority over depression, and declare that I am far from oppression, it shall not come near me. I live in peace and freedom from terror. No weapon formed against me shall prosper, and every tongue that rises against me in judgement, I condemn. I cancel every plan of the devil to steal, kill or destroy in my life! The law of the Spirit of life in Christ Jesus, has set me free from the law of sin and death. I am free from oppression, bondage, calamity, death and affliction. Christ has set me free to live a free life, I refuse to be entangled again in a yoke of bondage. So, I take my stand! Never again will I let anyone put a harness of slavery on me. I have the Holy Spirit living inside of me, and where the Spirit of the Lord is, there is freedom. Jesus has set me free, and I choose to walk in the glorious freedom that belongs to the children of God.

I AM VICTORIOUS OVER THE DEVIL

Scripture

You are of God, little children, and have overcome them, because He who is in you is greater than he who is in the world - 1 John 4:4.

Proclamation

I AM victorious! I belong to God and have conquered the devil and his demons. Jesus who lives in me is far greater than the devil and his agents who are in the world. On the cross, Jesus vanquished the devil, canceled the record of the charges against me and nailed it to the cross. He disarmed the spiritual rulers and authorities, and shamed them publicly. All my sins are forgiven, my slate is wiped clean, my old arrest warrant is canceled and nailed to Christ's cross. Anything the devil is trying to do in my life and family today cannot be done because of what Jesus already did on the cross 2000 years ago. Jesus's work is finished, complete, lavish, total, and eternal. I cannot be bound, poor, sick, fail, or be oppressed because Jesus has already healed, saved, delivered, and set me free. I am blessed; I cannot be cursed; I am healed; I cannot be sick; I am free; I cannot be bound; I am rich; I cannot be poor. I cannot be cursed, yoked, or defeated because of what Jesus did for me on the cross. I stand in all the finished works of Christ.

_____

_____

_____

_____

I AM SUPERNATURALLY FAVORED

Scripture

You have found favor, loving-kindness, and mercy in My sight and I know you personally and by name - Exodus 33:17.

Proclamation

I AM supernaturally favored! I have found favor in the sight of God, and He knows me by name. He has blessed me and surrounded me with His favor as a shield. The time for the manifestation of God's supernatural favor in my life, the appointed time, has come, and it is NOW! God's favor has set me apart, elevated me, announced me and positioned me. I have favor and good success in the sight of God and man. Goodness and mercy pursues me and overtakes me, all the days of my life. God has set a table before me in the presence of my enemies! He has anointed my head with oil, and my cup overflows! God's favor is working mightily in my life, opening doors, and making a way. His favor is for my entire lifetime. The night of weeping is over and joy has come this morning. Like Esther won favor and grace in the eyes of the king, I have received supernatural favor, grace, and honor; and God has set the royal crown of distinction, excellence and glory upon me. Like Jesus, I increase daily in wisdom, stature and favor with God and man.

I AM THE LIGHT OF THE WORLD

Scripture

"You are the light of the world, like a city on a hilltop that cannot be hidden - Matthew 5:14.

Proclamation

I AM the light of the world! Because Jesus lives in me, I have the light of life. I am like a city on a hilltop that cannot be hidden. My life is on display, like a letter skillfully crafted by God's hand for all to read. My light shines brightly and illuminates my world and sphere of influence. People who don't know God, can see Him in and through me. I will not hide my light, but will let it shine brightly before others so that everyone will see it and praise my heavenly Father. My light shines in the darkness, and the darkness can never extinguish it. God is light, and in Him is no darkness at all. As I walk with Him, I am flooded with and reflect His light, and the blood of Jesus continually cleanses me from all sin. God's shining light guides me in my daily choices and decisions; and the revelation of His word makes my pathway clear. I walk in the highway of light, and my path shines brighter and brighter until the full light of day. I declare that light overtakes darkness in every area of my life.

_____

_____

_____

_____

I AM GOD'S MASTERPIECE

Scripture

For we are God's masterpiece. He has created us anew in Christ Jesus, so we can do the good things he planned for us long ago - Ephesians 2:10.

Proclamation

I AM God's masterpiece! I see myself strong, healthy, talented, powerful, victorious, and living the abundant life Jesus purchased for me. I am God's expert workmanship, His work of art, created in Christ Jesus, reborn from above, spiritually transformed, renewed, and ready to be used for good works, which God prepared for me beforehand. I choose to walk in obedience and take the paths which God set, so that I would live the good life which He prearranged and made ready for me. God made all the delicate, inner parts of my body, and knit me together in my mother's womb. I am fearfully and wonderfully made. He saw me before I was born and every day of my life is recorded in His book. I go forth today to do the good works He has planned for me to do – to manifest His goodness and glory; to speak life instead of death, order instead of chaos, victory instead of defeat, mercy instead of judgement, love instead of the law. I am God's masterpiece and will fulfill His divine design for my life.

_____
_____
_____
_____

I AM HEALED

Scripture

He personally carried our sins in his body on the cross so that we can be dead to sin and live for what is right. By his wounds you are healed - 1 Peter 2:24.

Proclamation

I AM healed by the stripes of Jesus! I am healthy and whole, nothing missing, nothing broken! I choose to walk in divine health and healing daily! I oppose sickness in all its forms. I speak the Zoe life of God to every cell, tissue, organ, and system in my body. I declare that by the stripes of Jesus I was, and am healed. My salvation in Christ also included my deliverance, healing, restoration, and wholeness. I receive and appropriate them now. Spirit of infirmity, I bind you and declare that you have no place or authority in my life. I oppose, cancel, and reject heart disease, high cholesterol, cancer, high blood pressure, and every form of sickness from my life and body. I say NO to covid, infection, cold, flu, and allergies. I choose life, and declare that I walk in abundant life. No evil will conquer me; no disease will infect me, and no plague will come near my home. Jehovah Rophe is my divine health and healer. I am safe in Him.

_____
_____
_____
_____

I AM A FRIEND OF GOD

Scripture

I no longer call you slaves, because a master doesn't confide in his slaves. But I call you my most intimate and cherished friends since I have told you everything the Father told me – John 15:15.

Proclamation

I AM a friend of God! Jesus calls me His friend. When I was utterly helpless, Christ came at just the right time and died for me. Most people would not be willing to die for an upright person, but God showed his great love for me by sending Christ to die for me while I was still a sinner. I am a friend of God. My friendship with God was secured by the death of his Son, and now, I am saved through His life. I am not a friend of the world, because friendship with the world means enmity with God. I do not love the world, nor the things that are in it, because the love of the Father is in me. The world offers only a craving for physical pleasure, a craving for everything we see, and pride in our achievements and possessions. I say No to the world and Yes to God. I rejoice in my wonderful new relationship with God because my Lord Jesus Christ has made me a friend of God! Jesus is my friend that sticks closer than a brother.

_____

_____

_____

_____

AFTERWORD

The purpose of this book is to tear down wrong mindsets and measurements; execute a paradigm shift in your thinking, and adjust your lens to see yourself through the eyes of God. Your identity, worth and personal value do not depend on anything external, or what people say about you. Your identity and worth are intrinsic and rooted in your relationship with God. You have a purpose and destiny far greater than anything that happened to you. It doesn't matter what you have done or been through, how long you've been down, laid out, or piled upon. It doesn't matter how long you've been in the dark. You can begin again, TODAY. It's called redemption and His name is Jesus! God has a strategic move in your future that will restore all that you lost. God has anointed you to prosper and empowered you to succeed. You are in position - right place, right time, right people. God has kingdom connections and divine encounters all pre-arranged for you. You are on a collision course with destiny! But you must stay on track.

How do you stay on track? Philippians 3:3 provides the prescription. It states: "For we Christians are the true circumcision, who worship God in spirit and glory and pride ourselves in Jesus Christ, and put no confidence or dependence on what we are in the flesh, outward privileges, physical advantages and external appearances."

Here are the guard rails to help you stay on track:

1. Worship God in spirit and pray in the Holy Spirit.
2. Glory in Christ: Have your identity in Christ and Christ alone. Like apostle Paul who said, "But as for me, I will never boast about anything except the cross of our Lord Jesus Christ. The world has been crucified to me through the cross, and I to the world." (Galatians 6:14).
3. Put no confidence in the flesh - your flesh or any flesh. Put no confidence in your position, education, money, status, looks, performance, job or political affiliation. Put all your trust and confidence in God.

Be sure to put on your helmet. Your helmet of salvation is the knowledge of who you are in Christ, and it protects your mind from Satan's lies and deceptions.

NOTES

NOTES

NOTES

ACKNOWLEDGEMENTS

1. Every book is the result of the work of a team, and this book is no exception.

2. Thank You, to my friend and partner Holy Spirit, who helps me to pray and proclaim faithfully God's word and will.

3. Thanks to my children, Emmanuel, Timothy, and Rhema, whose support, encouragement and love keep me motivated.

4. Thanks to Mike Ancona who diligently reviewed the manuscript and provided valuable insights and edits.

5. Thanks to the pastor Mary Cooper for her diligent review of the manuscript, helpful comments and endorsement.

6. Thanks to pastor Kwaku Marfor for his diligent review of the manuscript, helpful comments and endorsement.

7. Thanks to John Radell, Chairman, Faith and Freedom Coalition, Mid Atlantic for his partnership in the work of the kingdom, diligent manuscript review and endorsement.

8. Thanks to Dr. Phyllis Arno, Co-Founder of National Christian Counselors Association, for her clinical supervision, diligent review of the manuscript, and endorsement.

9. Thanks to the GraceTalk Board, the *iDECLARE Prayer and Proclamation* Team, and the Racial Equity and Unity Team, whose partnership, leadership and support made our work and events so successful.

10. Thanks to Rae's Studios that diligently produced and edited the GraceTalk shows with excellence and uncommon skill.

11. Thanks to TJ our technical expert, for his excellent support, outstanding work ethic, and being an all-around amazing resource.

12. I am deeply grateful to God my Father, the Lord Jesus Christ, and the Holy Spirit for the privilege of prayer.

13. This book is a joint effort. I am truly grateful for the opportunity to partner with you all. I am better because of you.

14. To God be ALL the glory!

ENDNOTES

CHAPTER 1:

1. Choosing A Life of Victory, Gloria Godson, Xulon Press, 2019.

2. 10 Unbelievable Inheritance Stories, January 20, 2010, Marite, Oddee.

3. Single and Happy, Are You A W.H.O.L.E Single, Gloria Godson, Xulon Press, 2019.

CHAPTER 2:

1. Believer's Authority, Happy Caldwell, Whitaker House, 2013.

2. How a Fake Saudi Prince Conned Investors out of Nearly $8 Million, Tom Huddleston Jr., CNBC, January 8, 2020.

3. Insight for Living, Chuck Swindoll, 2017.

CHAPTER 3:

1. Indonesian Report Finds Fatal Lion Air Jet Crash Due to Boeing, Pilots, Maintenance, Willy Kurniawan, NBC News, October 25, 2019.

2. Merriam Webster's Dictionary.

3. Single and Happy, Are You A W.H.O.L.E Single, Gloria Godson, Xulon Press, 2019.

CHAPTER 4:

1. David Jeremiah, 23 Verses About the Goodness of God, davidjeremiah.org.
2. Single and Happy, Are You A W.H.O.L.E Single, Gloria Godson, Xulon Press, 2019.
3. Fight to Win with Prayer and Proclamations, Grivante Press, 2020.

CHAPTER 5:

1. Mistaken Identity: Two Families, One Survivor, Unwavering Hope, Don Van Ryn, Howard Books, 2009.
2. 25 Ways to Win with People, John Maxwell, Thomas Nelson, 2005.

CHAPTER 6:

1. What is the Definition of Grace? Got Questions.org.
2. Don Stewart, Is God righteous? Blueletterbible.org.
3. Temperament Theory, Richard G. Arno, Ph.D., 2018.

CHAPTER 7

1. Counseling the Co-Dependent: A Christian Perspective Utilizing Temperament; Jean M. LaCour, National Christian Counselors Association, 1996.

2. Spirit Controlled Temperament, Dr. Tim LaHaye, Tyndale House Publishers 1993.
3. Temperament Theory, Richard G. Arno, Ph.D., 2018.

CHAPTER 9

1. Single and Happy, Are You A W.H.O.L.E Single, Gloria Godson, Xulon Press, 2019.
2. Fight to Win with Prayer and Proclamations, Grivante Press, 2020.

CHAPTER 10

1. Choosing A Life of Victory, Gloria Godson, Xulon Press, 2019.
2. Single and Happy, Are You A W.H.O.L.E Single, Gloria Godson, Xulon Press, 2019.
3. Competing Worldviews Influence Today's Christians, Barna Group Research Release, May 9, 2017.

CHAPTER 14

1. Words of Life Ministries Bible Studies, Series 13, Study 7, The Marks of The Lord Jesus.
2. Rick Renner, "The Holy Spirit Is Our Seal and Guarantee, June 29, 2020.
3. Choosing A Life of Victory, Gloria Godson, Xulon Press, 2019.

CHAPTER 15

1. The Elephant and the Rope, A. M. Marcus, Createspace Independent Publishing Platform, 2015.

OTHER BOOKS BY THE AUTHOR

Reclaim Your Destiny, 31 Day Proclamations to Build Christ Esteem And Godly Self Image, *LifeWork Press, 2022*

The Colt Story, LifeWork Press, 2021

I AM The God Kind, Living in the Reality of Your Identity in Christ, LifeWork Press, 2021

Fight to Win with Prayer and Proclamations, LifeWork Press 2020.

Choosing a Life of Victory, Xulon Press 2019.

Single and Happy, Are You A W.H.O.L.E Single? Xulon Press 2019.

Single and Happy, Are You A W.H.O.L.E Single? Study Guide.

Workbook: 5 Practical Steps to Wholeness in Spirit, Soul, and Body.

ADDITIONAL RESOURCES BY THE AUTHOR

1. The Finished Works of Christ
2. What is in Your Mouth?
3. The Unstoppable God
4. Becoming Who You Are
5. 2019, Year of Accelerated Restoration
6. A Mighty Fortress Is Our God
7. The Firm Foundation
8. The Holy Spirit, my Friend & Partner
9. What Will You Sow in Your Life This Year?
10. A Woman of Character
11. Character Counts
12. Kingdom Prayer
13. Jesus is Praying for You
14. Praying the Names of God
15. Praying Through Ephesians
16. Alpha & Omega, The God of Time
17. The Ministry of Intercession
18. The Power of Prayer and Fasting

19. Sons of God, Who are They?

20. Does Jesus Value Women?

21. What is Your Nickname?

22. Altars and Priesthoods

23. Prayers in the Bible

24. The Release of His Power

25. Solitude – Alone with God

26. Curses, Covenants and How to Break Them

27. Proclamations, How Kings Rule

28. His Promise, You've Already Got It!

29. Hotliness, The Profile of Godly Singleness

AUTHOR MINISTRY RESOURCES

LIFEWORK MINISTRIES, INC.
LifeWork Ministries empowers people to live the abundant life in Christ. We preach, write, and witness! Our compelling mission is to release the Life of Christ into the world by using our faith, thinking our faith, speaking our faith, singing our faith, praying our faith and sharing our faith. Connect with us on our website: **www.lifeworkministries.org** or send us an email at **lifeworkministriesinc@gmail.com**

WEEKLY RADIO BROADCAST
Gloria has a weekly Bible teaching program on REACH Gospel Radio and the Wilkins Radio network. You can hear her radio broadcast in cities across America. For the schedule of her weekly radio bible teaching program, please go to our website: **www.lifeworkministries.org.**

LICENSED CLINICAL PASTORAL COUNSELOR & TEMPERAMENT COUNSELOR
At LifeWork Ministries, we provide individual, family, marriage, pre-marital, relationship, career, ministry, and teen counseling. Contact us on our website at **www.lifeworkministries.org**

iDECLARE PRAYER AND PROCLAMATION
Gloria hosts the iDECLARE Prayer and Proclamation event. The word of God, spoken in faith, is the most powerful weapon known to man. At iDECLARE, we load, cock, and fire the word of God to transform our lives, families, and nations!

RACIAL EQUITY & UNITY
Gloria leads the Biblical Equity and Unity (BEU) collaborative, hosts the monthly BEU Community dialogue and the annual Racial Equity and Unity luncheon. Our vision is to educate, engage, and advocate

on issues of biblical equity and unity; and to promote racial reconciliation and healing. Facebook@REUofDE.

SAVED SINGLES SUMMIT

Gloria hosts the Saved Singles Summit, a premier Christ-centered forum, which brings together Christian singles from churches across America for a time of fun, fellowship, empowerment, kingdom connections and new opportunities. Join us at: **www.savedsinglessummit.com**. Facebook@savedsinglessummit.

SINGLE CHRISTIANS CONNECT MEETUP GROUPS

For clean, fun, weekly activities and social events.
https://www.meetup.com/single-christians-connect/
https://www.meetup.com/philadelphia_single_Christians-connect/

SINGLE SENSE CONVERSTIONS

Monthly fun, interactive, Zoom panel discussion on singles issues, every 4th Friday.

THE GRACETALK

Weekly internet talk show hosted by Gloria on Sundays at 6pm:
https://www.facebook.com/TheGraceTalk/live_videos/

ABOUT THE AUTHOR

Gloria Godson is a multi-faceted corporate executive, with an illustrious career in the Energy Industry. She is a visionary, thought and strategy leader, and consummate senior executive. An attorney by training, she rose through several executive leadership positions to become a Vice President in Exelon Corporation, the largest energy company in America.

Most importantly, Gloria is a Christian leader, Bible teacher, author, prayer minister, and conference speaker. She is a Licensed Clinical Pastoral Counselor, Certified Temperament Counselor and Professional Clinical Member of the National Christian Counselors Association. She is the CEO of LifeWork Ministries, and has a weekly Bible teaching radio program. She hosts Wholeness Workshops, Temperament Workshops, the premier annual Saved Singles Summit, the iDECLARE Prayer and Proclamation event, the Racial Equity and Unity Community Events, and the live *GraceTalk* internet talk show.

Gloria served on the Board of Word of Life (WOL) Christian Center in Newark, Delaware, a full gospel, non-denominational church, for over twelve years. And for over fifteen years, Gloria also served as overseer of the WOL prayer ministries, and is a regular eye witness to God's miraculous answers to prayer. She is a powerful minister of the word of God, with a singular focus on building lives and the kingdom of God. She is a dynamic speaker who connects with both professional and Christian audiences across the country and around the world.

Gloria loves to serve her community! She is on the Board of Faith and Freedom Coalition Mid-Atlantic. Gloria is an online missionary with Global Media Outreach, a dedicated volunteer with the REACH community outreach, the Sunday Breakfast Mission, Urban Promise, Exceptional Care for Children, and more. She loves God passionately and believes in the unstoppable power of Almighty God to do the impossible. She has three children and lives in Delaware, United States.

AUTHOR CONTACT

To invite Gloria to speak, send her your prayer request, place a book order, or simply connect, please go to:

www.lifeworkministries.org

www.gloriagodson.com

Facebook@TheGraceTalk

Instagram@TheGraceTalk

YouTube@TheGraceTalk

LifeWork Ministries, Inc.

P. O. Box 56,

Townsend, DE 19734

www.lifeworkministries.org

EMAIL

lifeworkministriesinc@gmail.com

www.ingramcontent.com/pod-product-compliance
Lightning Source LLC
LaVergne TN
LVHW040140080526
838202LV00042B/2963